To Jessie and Lee

Part of the production cost of this volume was contributed
by the Bill Sample Memorial Fund of the San Mateo chapter,
National Association of Social Workers, as a tribute
to Bill Sample's professional skills and dedication to social work.

The research reported in this book
was supported by grants Nos. 090 and H-68
from the Social and Rehabilitation
Service, U.S. Department of Health,
Education, and Welfare.

International Standard Book Number: 0–87101–619–2
Library of Congress Catalog Card Number: 72–80476
Printed in the U.S.A.
 3

An Experiment in the
Organization of Work Groups

THE MIDWAY OFFICE

by Edward E. Schwartz and William C. Sample
with the collaboration of Shirley A. Star and Claire M. Anderson

NATIONAL ASSOCIATION OF SOCIAL WORKERS, INC.
2 PARK AVENUE, NEW YORK, NEW YORK 10016
PRICE: $9.00

CONTENTS

FOREWORD

The Midway Project was a commitment, an experiment, and a prophecy. Few modern prophecies are as immediately and demonstrably validated as those found in this book that says in effect: The social work profession will have to face current and future manpower problems by better task analysis, classification differentiation, cost-benefit evaluation, and other management techniques.

Today the social work profession scrambles to meet its detractors' criticisms and its dedicated practitioners' concerns for professional accountability. The attempt to bring an efficient system to the organization of social services—now proceeding along a chaotic but inevitable path—is the major task before the profession and the National Association of Social Workers. If only the profession had heeded the prophecies of this project and the concerns reported by Dr. Schwartz at the Second NASW Professional Symposium on Human Services and Professional Responsibility in 1968.[1]

The project, which is the subject of this book, illustrates the classic pattern of problems encountered in research projects. If there were no significant outcomes, the documentation and analysis of data alone would make it required reading in every school of social work and the subject of scrutiny by every practitioner. That the hypotheses concerning staff morale, staff activity, and client change produced such different and important outcomes makes the book even more intriguing.

---

1. *See* Edward E. Schwartz, ed., *Planning, Programming, Budgeting Systems (PPBS) and Social Welfare* (Chicago: School of Social Service Administration, University of Chicago, 1970).

The National Association of Social Workers is publishing this book as part of its commitment to find, select, and publish materials that make a significant contribution to the profession. It is hoped that by its publication, the profession will be stimulated to deal vigorously with the serious management and practice problems it so amply documents.

CHAUNCEY A. ALEXANDER, ACSW
Executive Director
National Association of Social Workers

May 1972

ACKNOWLEDGMENTS

Contrary to the practice usually followed in jointly authored works, this acknowledgment is signed by only one author. For William C. Sample this volume is published posthumously. As assistant director of the Midway Project, he participated in planning the field experiment and was immediately responsible for the training of the experimental team supervisors and the social work analysts, supervision of the research staff, monitoring the experimental control procedures, and, indeed, for the entire day-to-day operation of the field experiment. Chapter 4 of this report draws heavily on his doctoral dissertation, which he had completed only shortly before his sudden death tragically cut short a most promising and already productive career. Bill's easy, discursive, and sometimes anecdotal style has withstood the rigors of collaborative research and the imperatives of editing and it persists in much of the material on client change.

Shirley A. Star served as chief consultant to the entire research staff on survey research methods and collaborated closely with Bill Sample in the collection, processing, and analysis of the data on client change. Here I add my thanks to Bill's frequent and fervent expressions of gratitude for her bountiful and most effective assistance throughout the project.

Claire M. Anderson was one of six doctoral candidates (including Bill Sample) who completed doctoral dissertations related to the Midway Project. Her research on formal and informal communication among Midway field staff workers added a dimension of her own creation to the project and one that was not contemplated at the time the research was designed. After completing her own work, she accepted responsibility for coordinating and controlling the processing of the various series of data collected in the course of the Midway field experiment. She also collaborated in the analysis of the work measurement data reported in Chapter 3. Of a relatively large number of persons who worked on the Midway Project at one time or another, she was one of the few who persisted to the—in some ways—bitter end.

Hirobumi Uno's dissertation on time study methods and work patterns of public assistance workers provided essential points of reference and background for our other work measurement data. He also contributed to data collection and analysis beyond that required for his own dissertation.

Thomas Carlsen's skillful analysis of the relationship between the morale and the work measurement data helped immeasurably in our efforts to pull together and interpret the various discrete strands of our statistical data.

James Gripton, who came to the Midway Project from the School of Social Work, University of Toronto, designed and was immediately responsible for the administration of the questionnaires on staff attitudes and morale. His doctoral dissertation was the chief source for Chapter 2 on changes in staff morale.

Dee Kilpatrick's doctoral dissertation was a spin-off of the Midway Project. He formulated his research problem after the field experiment in the Midway office was designed and under way. He first explored the use of data already collected in this project. Finding them to be insufficient for his purpose, he drew a sample of cases under care in the Midway office and conducted the interviews that were needed to produce the data required to meet the specific needs of his research. His dissertation constituted an important portion of the final report to the Children's Bureau of research conducted with support from Children's Bureau Grant WA-CB-H-68, which was administered jointly with funds received specifically for the Midway Project.

Dee Kilpatrick had come to the Midway Project as one of the six social work analysts who conducted and wrote up the social studies, both baseline and follow-up, and made the judgments from which were derived scores of direction and extent of client change. The other social work analysts and supporting members of the research staff who made substantial contributions to the conduct of the research included Leona Cain, Robert Friel, Esther Golber, Faith Jones, Bertice McDonald, Catherine Roherty, and Joan Wallace (analysts) and Paula Berger, Carol Butler, Albert Cook, Barbara Davis, Kathryn Gottschalk, Cleatris Henderson, Philip Hyde, Louis Richard Lessor, Mary

McMorris, Jimmie Reed, Ann Rothschild, Rose Watson, and Beatrice Williams (supporting staff). The social work analysts represented the project's most strategic and valuable research instruments. Their dedication and skill in the most difficult of working situations exceeded our expectations, and we stand in their debt. The supporting staff became imbued with the same esprit de corps and they succeeded to a surprising degree in maintaining their humanity while coping with and subduing highly programmed and mechanized procedures.

After the completion of the project the research staff reached an early and most plausible consensus to the effect that, if nothing else, we had proved that it was possible to conduct a controlled field experiment in the midst of the kind of maelstrom commonly known as a district office of a public assistance agency. For this achievement we are greatly indebted to the members of the organization we were studying—the Cook County Department of Public Aid. Although we could not agree with the department's director, the late Raymond Hilliard, on many important matters, we register our admiration for his courage in opening his department to outside scrutiny and his fidelity to the agreement he made with us.

We are most grateful to the entire field staff of the Midway office for their almost cheerful willingness to serve—as some of them were wont to express it—as the "guinea pigs" in this experiment and especially to the supervising caseworkers who bore the brunt of the direct demands of the research on the field staff. On Pearl Rosenzweig, the supervisor of the Midway District Office, fell the onus of working through with us the myriad of trying problems that arose. The course of our relationship with her achieved the heights and plumbed the depths of an exquisitely ambivalent love-hate relationship, with love, of course, triumphing in the end, and we emerged with the greatest of admiration for her personal integrity and her professional accomplishments.

The Midway Project was extensive, prolonged, and expensive. The chief financial costs were borne by the U.S. Department of Health, Education, and Welfare through its Social and Rehabilitation Service, and its predecessor and constituent units, including the Social Service Administration, the Welfare Administration, and the Children's Bureau. In addition to the standard acknowledgments to these organizations, we wish to thank Ida Merriam,

James Cowhig, and Charles Gershenson for their interest in our research and their patient support in the face of our grievous shortcomings or, perhaps more accurately, "longcomings." The Wieboldt Foundation assisted us with a "wind-up" grant, and in this connection we wish to recognize the good offices of Robert MacRae.

We received invaluable public support at critical junctures from our Advisory Committee. We were also the grateful beneficiaries of counsel on research strategies and techniques during the planning of the research from a technical subcommittee consisting of Peter Blau, Philip Hauser, Morris Janowitz, and Fred Strodtbeck, all of the University of Chicago.

The following colleagues in the School of Social Service Administration responded to requests for assistance on special assignments: Ernestina Alexander consulted on the training of members of the research staff in the making of judgments based on social study data. Bernice Simon provided in-service training to supervisors and assistant district office supervisors on how to give and use case consultation and to differentiate it from supervisory control. Arthur Schwartz led a student group through a validity check of our method of analyzing client outcomes. We were helped toward closure by Robert Weagant, then associate dean, who ironed out some administrative wrinkles, and by John Schuerman, who provided consultation on some final statistical problems. In the end the senior author was able to complete this work because of the generous protection against many of the customary demands of membership in a faculty of a school of social work provided by Ralph Garber, dean of the George Warren Brown School of Social Work, Washington University.

The list of acknowledgments grows embarrassingly long for so modest a production, and the final bow is for another bitter-ender, Miss Jimmie Reed, the Midway Project secretary, whose invaluable contributions lay not only in keeping the files and in typing the copy but also in enduring the research director and senior author. The final expression of sentiment must be the customary breast-beating and self-immolation: For all sins of omission and commission in this report, *mea culpa*.

EDWARD E. SCHWARTZ

St. Louis, Missouri

Chapter One

BACKGROUND AND PLAN

The manpower shortage has been one of the major concerns of social work practitioners and welfare administrators since the rapid growth of public relief agencies in the depression of the 1930s. During the subsequent decades and into the 1960s, although speculation was rife and opinions on how to solve the problem were freely offered, little research was conducted on the matter and little systematically acquired knowledge was available. The purpose of the project that is the subject of this book (hereinafter called the Midway Project)—a field experiment conducted in the Midway District Office of the Cook County (Illinois) Department of Public Aid—was to develop and test ways of improving the organization and use of public assistance personnel. Public assistance was the field selected for this research because in recent decades it has been the major source of employment of social workers in the United States.

Review of the literature on social welfare manpower and observation of the efforts of the social work profession and of social welfare organizations to deal with the manpower problem revealed an almost exclusive focus on staff recruitment and training to the nearly total neglect of improving utilization of available manpower. In the authors' view more efficient utilization of personnel would assist not only in reducing the manpower shortage but also in improving the general effectiveness of social welfare administration, regardless of the state of the labor market.

The research staff of the Midway Project was based in a graduate school of social work—the School of Social Service Administration of the University of Chicago (SSSA)—and the staff were first impressed with the problems attendant to employment of the school's graduates in public assistance programs. Like some other schools of social work, SSSA has worked over the years for the professionalization of public welfare programs, including those administering public assistance. The policy of the Cook County Department of Public Aid (hereinafter referred to as the department), as with many other public agencies, was to increase the number of social workers on its staff. A substantial number of stipends for graduate study had been awarded to the department's employees in return for a commitment by each recipient to serve the department for a specified number of years following graduation. However, the experience here—as elsewhere in the country—has been that a relatively small proportion of such workers remain after fulfilling their commitment.

In a social welfare manpower survey made in 1960, public assistance agencies reported that the percentage of workers having any graduate social work study had not only failed to increase during the previous decade, but had actually declined.[1] In 1950 the figure was 22 percent; in 1960, 17 percent. At both measuring points the percentage of public welfare employees with professional social work degrees was 4 percent.

Discussions with former students and other social workers with recent employment experience in public assistance, as well as the authors' observations, led us to believe that social workers are not attracted to, or tend to leave, public assistance employment in large part because of the incongruity between the values and culture of the social work profession and the more or less latent goals of many of the organizations in which public assistance programs are administered.

---

1. *Salaries and Working Conditions of Social Welfare Manpower in 1960,* survey conducted by the U.S. Department of Labor, Bureau of Labor Statistics, in cooperation with the National Social Welfare Assembly and the U.S. Department of Health, Education, and Welfare (New York: National Social Welfare Assembly, 1961). Comparable national survey data were not collected for 1970.

The aim of the Midway Project was, however, not merely to improve the lot of the professional social worker in public assistance, but rather to fashion and test a way of working that would be more rewarding for the entire staff in contact with clients, would provide needed services more effectively, and would be more acceptable to the informed community. Focus was on the organization of work at the point of service delivery—that is, on the worker and his immediate supervisor.

DEFINING THE PROBLEM

The conventional form of work organization in a large urban public assistance agency at the point of service delivery can be described in a general way as follows: An applicant is seen by an intake worker. If he is found eligible for financial assistance, his case is assigned to a fieldworker. The assignment may be made by a supervisor, but the case is given to the worker assigned to the geographic area in which the client lives. The worker assumes primary responsibility for making decisions about financial assistance and other welfare services and for providing such services or making them available to the client.

The nature and extent of the supervisor's involvement in service delivery may vary among agencies, within different parts of the same agency, and for the same supervisor over a period of time. A supervisor may perform a number of roles—as manager, consultant, trainer, and caseworker. Observations made by the project staff before completing the experimental design suggested that department supervisors, in fact, functioned chiefly as managerial-control officers. Most of the supervisory time spent on specific cases seemed to be given to reviewing work already performed by fieldworkers and to discussing problems arising from this work. Little supervisory time seemed to be spent on planning what was to be done in specific cases and even less on direct treatment services. Supervisors rarely had direct contact with clients except in grave emergencies or when substituting for absent workers. Caseworker supervisors were also responsible for workers' personal evaluations, for assisting in orienting newly assigned workers, and for learning, transmitting, and interpreting rules and regulations of the Central Administrative Office. In Cook County the more recently appointed supervisors were professionally qualified, but those with more seniority were not, and the latter were in the large majority.[2]

It seemed, somewhat ironically, that both workers and their supervisors were placed in positions in which they were required to invest most of their time in work for which they were not specifically prepared. The large majority of workers in the department who saw clients were college graduates without graduate degrees—or any other degrees—in social work.

Social workers who return with master's degrees from graduate schools of social work quickly qualify for promotion and move into supervisory positions. Because the social work master's curriculum does not as a rule prepare students for casework supervision, the new graduates again found themselves in positions for which they are not adequately prepared and that at the same time failed to make appropriate use of their educational background or developing practice skills. The reason they commonly gave for resigning their positions was usually "To accept a position in a setting where I can really use my educational background, become a more competent social worker, and make a professional contribution."

The administrative problem to which the Midway Project was addressed is whether available personnel can be more effectively utilized than at present in the provision of public assistance services. Public assistance services are seen as including both financial payments and other social services. The researchers were of the opinion that control of financial assistance was currently receiving a disproportionate amount of the time and attention of public assistance agencies and that it was desirable to concentrate on the improvement of preventive and rehabilitative services to individuals and families.

The most general form of the research problem was to test the

2. For purposes of this research professional qualification for social work is defined simply as possession of a graduate degree from an accredited school of social work. The term "social worker" is reserved for those with such qualifications. The terms "social welfare worker," "welfare worker," or "staff worker" are used specifically for employees without such qualifications or collectively for those with and without such qualifications.

proposition that the efficiency of the administration of public assistance services can be increased by increasing the specialization of work in the provision of service. A classical tenet of organizational theory is that an increase in division of labor or specialization results in an increased need for coordination. The need for coordination is especially high when human services are involved, and the solution of the coordinating problem tends to be complex. The second and more specific theoretical formulation was that a team form of organization would both increase the opportunities for specialization of members of the work group and at the same time provide for increased coordination through supervisory control.

Attention was first directed to the design of a supervisory position that would be more suitable and satisfying for social workers. The researchers then sought to reconstruct the related worker position so that it would come closer to filling the needs and using the capabilities of people in these jobs than it had in the past.

The researchers were especially concerned with the plight of new recruits, who were predominantly recent young college graduates. Some had been unsuccessful in finding jobs elsewhere that interested them or in which they performed proficiently. Most wanted to "work with people" and were highly motivated to "do something"—to be effective and constructive. Many tended to be alienated rather quickly by the heavy bureaupathology endemic to the department. The rules and regulations governing the administration of assistance were so detailed as to fill several volumes of mimeographed releases. These were expanded and otherwise amended so frequently and the interrelationships between regulations are so complex that it was not possible for the department to provide all workers with an up-to-date manual. After a short—quite mechanical and highly inadequate—orientation period, focused chiefly on the use of forms relating to family income and assistance payments, new recruits were assigned to a district office and almost immediately made responsible for a field caseload of 90–100 or more cases.

One of the researchers' concerns was to define the fieldworkers' job in a way that would make the assumption of responsibility by new workers realistic. We were not in a position to modify the impact of insensitive or punitive policy on young workers who were trying to help clients, but we believed that we could buffer the impact of the work load and make the worker's induction into the organization less painful.

The worker who came into the organization with a bachelor's degree was not seen as developing into a professional social worker merely through the passage of time or even with carefully graduated experience and coaching from the casework supervisor. A situation was envisaged in which the new worker would gain proficiency in a series of specified tasks. His growth would be represented by an increasingly wide repertoire of tasks of increasing complexity, carried out under supervision of an increasingly more general nature. Workers with higher levels of aspiration and with the necessary qualifications would be encouraged to obtain professional social work education.

SETTING UP THE MIDWAY OFFICE

An agreement was reached between SSSA and the Cook County Department of Public Aid to establish and operate a research and training office on a cooperative basis. This office, to be known as the Midway District Office, was to provide needed public assistance services to the community, but would be differentiated from other district offices in that its management was to be directed primarily not toward its own immediate operating efficiency but rather toward the contribution that it might make through research and through the provision of fieldwork training for graduate social work students. The department agreed to provide service staff to man the office, to take responsibility for its general administration, and to provide space, office equipment, and other facilities. SSSA agreed to staff and direct the research and training operations.[3]

The purpose of setting up a special office was to create a facility for conducting a field experiment. One of the research

3. As it was set up, the office provided for a number of field placement units for students in the master's program and their supervisors. This aspect of the Midway Project was independent of the research program and is not discussed in this report.

advantages of a field experiment, as compared with laboratory or simulated research, is the opportunity for and necessity of dealing with real-life situations. A considerable amount of organization theory regarding group behavior in administrative settings is based on laboratory experimentation. However, there is little evidence and increasing skepticism regarding the transferability of the findings of this kind of research to the organizational situation. For this reason it was agreed that the Midway District Office (hereinafter referred to as the Midway office) would operate under the rules and regulations of the department that pertained to other district offices. An additional advantage of this decision was that it resulted in the department's official approval, cooperation, and provision of resources. However, the project staff reserved the right to petition for exceptions to rules or regulations that in our opinion would jeopardize the integrity of the research.

| Location and Clientele |

The area served by the Midway office was on the South Side of Chicago and included the Hyde Park neighborhood, in which the University of Chicago is located, and the Kenwood and Woodlawn neighborhoods. This district comprised parts of two contiguous districts, and the clients residing within the newly delineated district were transferred to the Midway office.

The great majority of the transferred clients lived in Woodlawn, a community with a high proportion of black residents.[4] Woodlawn is a low-income area, but not the poorest in the city. The transferred caseload consisted of about 3,200 cases, half of which were receiving Aid to Families with Dependent Children, including families in which the head of the household was unemployed, or general assistance. The remaining caseload consisted of clients without children receiving general assistance

4. The Hyde Park–Kenwood communities contain a number of middle-income and some upper-income families as well as a scattering of families and individuals dependent on public assistance. These communities contain both black and white residents. They were included in the district not so much in the interests of research as to provide the students placed in the Midway office with a varied field practice experience.

grants and the special types of public assistance for individuals.

| Staffing |

The staff of the Midway office was obtained from the staff of other district offices of the department, largely by voluntary transfers. Personnel were selected by the district office supervisor, who had a wide acquaintance with department staff throughout the county and who performed an outstanding recruitment job in the tight labor market of 1962. The plan was to obtain the best staff possible through the established personnel channels of the department without unduly depleting other district offices.

Although an attempt was made to portray the Midway office as a laboratory rather than a model office, it was the researchers' initial impression that the idea of working in connection with a university-sponsored research project was attractive to a number of supervisors and workers who were highly motivated to serve clients and who hoped that the conditions to be established in the office would make this possible. It was later discovered that a number of recruits had been contemplating entering graduate school and saw employment with the Midway Project as an experience that might facilitate their admission to a school of social work. The subsequent resignation of some of these people during the course of the experiment therefore resulted from turnover factors peculiar to the Midway office.

| Level of Service |

Another unanticipated consequence of the publicly expressed emphasis on the experimental nature of the Midway office was covert but rather definite indications of fear in the community, expressed in the form of questions about what kind of experiments were going to be performed on whom.[5] The term "experimental" was immediately dropped and the researchers made it clear that clients would not be used as guinea pigs. In discussions with various other interested parties we also made clear our intent to conduct a field experiment that would not place any of

5. In retrospect this feeling can be seen as one of the early examples of the later well-known reaction of black ghetto populations against their selection as guinea pigs for "overstudy" by the white establishment.

the participants—clients or staff—in a less desirable position than they would be in if the experiment were not to be conducted.

As it turned out, this apparently simple formula was more difficult to apply in practice than had initially been assumed. The research design did not provide for the withholding of service from anyone. Rather than using control cases as defined in classical experimental design, comparison cases were used. The comparison cases would receive services administered in the conventional way. The difficulty came in defining what was "conventional" in a department characterized by an extremely wide range of practices and situations.

To avoid the metaphysical or even the probabilistic difficulties in deciding what service a client would have received if the Midway office had not been established and at the same time to protect both the interests of the clients and the integrity of the experiment, the researchers decided that each client would be given the best service possible given the resources of the district office and within the requirements of the experimental design, but that in no case should a client be subjected to danger or hardship because of the requirements of the research. The Midway office was planned and organized to provide services at a high level relative to those provided in other district offices—not so much for purposes of demonstration, but rather on the assumption that it would be more feasible to detect variations among different types of services if at least some registered at the upper range of a quality scale than if they all clustered around zero.

DESIGN OF THE EXPERIMENT

The reasons for the decision to conduct a field experiment rather than an exploratory, descriptive-analytic, operational research, demonstration, or some other type of study were based on a number of considerations.[6] The researchers were aware of the opinion that experimentation should be attempted only when a problem

6. This section draws on Edward E. Schwartz, "Strategies for Research in Public Welfare Administration: The Field Experiment," *Trends in Social Work Practice and Knowledge* (New York: National Association of Social Workers, 1966), pp. 164–178.

is well structured, the variables have been clearly identified and defined, the potency of the experimental input is established, instrumentation of the measurement criteria has been perfected, the field and study subjects are under control, the risks are known, and so on. Although it was agreed that this view might be correct for the physical and technological sciences, we also believed that it needed to be modified for field experiments designed to test administrative innovation. It was hoped that a field experiment—with its necessary planning and pilot studies, its possible spin-offs and follow-ups—might develop into a continuing program of discrete but articulated studies whose findings might provide a cumulative fund of knowledge aimed at the improvement of public welfare policy and administration. Nor were the researchers insensible to the opportunities that this kind of experience would provide for the training of doctoral students in research. Few field experiments had been or were being attempted in social welfare and the researchers knew of none in public assistance that had been reported since the pioneer effort of Simon and others in 1941.[7]

Observations over time of the evanescent quality of the evidence on which changes in practice were based convinced the researchers of the desirability of at least an occasional corrective in the form of a quest, if not for certainty, at least for "satisficing" evidence, to use Simon's term. The then newly established Cooperative Research Program of the Social Security Board, with its administrative emphasis on the desirability of "hard," theoretically oriented, controlled experimentation, supported our thinking and interests and moved us in the direction of a field experiment.

| Staff Organization |

The experiment was designed to permit comparisons of the operation, at the point of service delivery, of a conventionally organized public assistance staff with a staff organized in a way intended to produce results that would be preferable from the point of view

7. Herbert A. Simon, W. R. Divine, E. M. Cooper, and Milton Chernin, *Determining Work Loads for Professional Staff in a Public Welfare Agency* (Berkeley: University of California, Bureau of Public Administration, 1941).

of professional social work. All sixty members of the Midway field staff were organized into ten work groups under two plans, designated Plan A and Plan B. The two plans were operated simultaneously and can be regarded as two parallel experiments.

Plan A was a high-caseload situation (ninety cases per worker), with managerial supervision and present service level expectation. Two conventional work groups, each consisting of a supervisor and five workers served by central filing and clerical staff, and two experimental teams, each also consisting of a supervisor and five workers, with each team served by a unit clerk, made up this plan.

Plan B was a low-caseload situation (forty-five cases per worker), with professional supervision and elevated service level expectation. Comprising it were three conventional work groups and three experimental teams, set up the same as the Plan A work groups and teams.

The experimental variable in both plans was the team form of field staff organization. The research was focused on the effects of changing the form of the field staff organization and not on the effects of caseload reduction. The reason for the parallel experiments will be explained later (see pages 14–16).

The experimental input—the experimental team—was not a monolithic element. Rather, it was a combination of factors that, taken together, define the structure of the work group and the way it operates. The objective in structuring the experimental teams was (1) to use the best social work judgment available in each work group in directing the total group effort toward the most effective provision of welfare services and (2) to provide an opportunity for each staff member to participate and to contribute at the upper limits of his capabilities, with appropriate controls to safeguard the interests of the clients and the community.

Plan B will be described first. The experimental input was developed around a restructuring of the duties and responsibilities of the supervisor and the worker. The first step in this restructuring was to place with the professional social worker responsibilities that would make full use of his educational background.

The frequently advanced notion of defining the social worker's job on the basis of the kind of client, difficulty or problem, or emergency nature of the situation was rejected as a basis for identifying the essentially professional component. Instead the idea of professional function was adopted, which was defined, in relation to specific cases, as including (1) study, (2) diagnosis, (3) case classification, (4) the laying out of the treatment plan, (5) administration of the treatment plan through supervision and direction of workers, (6) provision of direct treatment when considered appropriate because of the need to establish a treatment relationship, to assume responsibility in grave emergencies or crisis situations, or for other reasons, (7) change of diagnosis, case classification, or treatment plan as appropriate. The social work supervisors were, of course, also expected to perform such agency-required duties as instructing workers in agency rules and regulations and maintaining administrative controls.

The supervisor's job was to accept and retain direct responsibility for all cases assigned to him and to delegate specific tasks, rather than cases, to his workers. The supervisor was encouraged to look for appropriate opportunities to assign to two or more workers tasks to be performed simultaneously in relation to a given family and also to intervene directly in the treatment of a client when in his judgment such action was indicated.

The worker's function was seen as that of a technician performing "specific tasks, some comparatively elementary, others of greater complexity, but all of which are functional parts of the work of the professional person." [8] The role of the worker was therefore seen as that of assistant to the supervisor, with responsibility for carrying out tasks relating to the treatment of the client and his family, as assigned by the supervisor, and for reporting to the supervisor through case-recording and discussion.

A task is a time-limited unit of service provided by a field staff member to a client and involves one or more interviews, exclusive of intra-agency conferences. Examples of tasks are redeterminations of eligibility, assisting an evicted family to find temporary shelter, counseling a parent regarding an unmarried

8. Seymour Wolfbein, "Technicians and the Utilization of Professional Manpower," in *Proceedings of a Conference on the Utilization of Scientific and Professional Manpower* (New York: Columbia University Press, 1954), p. 49.

pregnant daughter, and referring a pregnant girl to needed medical and social services. The supervisor operationalized the treatment plan by assigning parts of it as tasks or episodes of service to be performed by different members of the team.

As part of the effort to enable the team worker, like the supervisor, to perform at his highest level of knowledge and skill, an attempt was made to relieve the worker as well as the supervisor of as much repetitive paperwork, telephoning, and other clerical activities as possible by placing responsibility for these with the unit clerk assigned to each team. The unit clerk was given duties that made minimal demands on initiative or exercise of judgment, such as posting information from more than one source to a single form, filing records, operating a "tickler" file, and such secretarial duties as answering the telephone, supplying simple, objective, and standardized information, receiving visitors, and taking messages. The job requirements and salary were correspondingly low. (Unit clerks with dependents were not appreciably better off than recipients of public aid.) The unit clerk was immediately responsible to the work group supervisor.

The objective in restructuring the supervisor's job was to increase his autonomy, influence, and effectiveness because the research was designed to test the effects of increasing the exercise of professional knowledge and judgment vis-à-vis the exercise of bureaucratic control at the point of service delivery. An attempt was also being made to test the effects of increasing the supervisor's involvement in direct treatment and strengthening his decision-making functions in the allocation and utilization of staff resources. The specialization of the work group was to be flexibly used; division of labor was to be utilized in simplifying the induction of new members into the work group, but the job of the more experienced worker would be continuously enlarged to call on his developing capacities. The increased need for coordination anticipated as a result of increased division of labor was to be met by the supervisor's retention of immediate authority for treatment of families and individuals rather than by allowing such authority to devolve hierarchically to the workers.

For want of a more descriptive term, the restructured work group is referred to as an "experimental team." This was not an interdisciplinary or an interprofessional team, nor was it intended to be a collegial group. The supervisor was formally responsible for the work of the team. The extent and nature of worker participation and group process in decision-making was left to be worked out among the members of each team. The team model was seen as being derived from the medical-clinical model, with the supervisor as the agent of the organization taking responsibility for the care of the client (patient) and with workers as technicians to assist him in administering the treatment he prescribes.

The research was designed, then, to measure differential outcomes of providing public assistance services under the customary or conventional work group form of organization and under the experimental team form of organization. Previous research, notably that of Heyman, had clearly indicated the feasibility and advantages of using the casework assistant in a clinical setting.[9] In the research of Heyman and others on the differential use of staff, the ratio of assistants to social workers varied between one to one and one to five—that is, one assistant to five social workers —with the assistant sometimes being immediately responsible to a supervisor of the other caseworkers. In the public assistance setting, however, the problem was not to introduce technical workers into a highly professionalized organization, but rather to establish effective professional controls over technical workers already operating within a highly bureaucratic organization. The project's aim of alleviating the manpower shortage could not be achieved—at least not directly—by increasing the ratio of already scarce professional personnel to more readily available technical personnel. It was decided, therefore, to retain the ratio of workers to supervisors already prevalent in the department, namely, five to one.

| Varying Caseloads |

A critical decision that had to be made in planning the experiment was the caseload the work groups were to carry. The average caseload in the department in 1962 was ninety cases. A

---

9. Margaret Heyman, "A Study of Effective Use of Social Workers in a Hospital: Selected Findings and Conclusions," *Social Service Review,* Vol. 35, No. 4 (December 1961), pp. 414–429.

controlling premise in this research, and one that influenced the choice of the field experiment as the research method, was that results would be most readily transferable to practice if obtained under conditions that were widely prevalent and that promised to persist. Inasmuch as high caseloads have been generally characteristic of public assistance administration since the passage of the Social Security Act in 1936, the researchers were forced to consider assigning the standard caseload.

On the other hand, such an assignment would place an extremely high demand on supervisors of experimental teams, each of whom would then be immediately and directly responsible for 450 cases. It was also believed that workers in conventional work groups would find it most difficult to recognize and meet even the more obvious and easily satisfied needs of clients if they had to deal with ninety cases containing a high proportion of individuals presenting considerable social pathology.

Since the researchers had no way of knowing what average caseloads would be in the future, it was decided therefore to test the team form of organization simultaneously under conditions of high and low caseload. For the high-caseload test, termed Plan A, the prevailing standard of ninety cases was retained. For the low-caseload test, Plan B, the caseload was set at forty-five cases.[10] Later the Bureau of Family Services of the Welfare Administration promulgated a standard of sixty-five cases so, as it turned out, the two caseload standards rather neatly straddled the national standard.

Although it would have made for a more elegant research design to test the team form of work organization in exactly the same form under conditions of both high and low caseload, it was decided that the original team model would have to be adapted to the field demands of a high-caseload situation. This was first attempted by modifying the service expectations. For the supervisor with 450 cases, continuation of the prevailing or "present" level of services was suggested. This was defined as chiefly providing financial assistance, responding to clients' re-

10. Given an upper limit of approximately 3,000 cases, which had been obtained for the Midway district, the decision on number of workers per group and on caseload limited the project to six groups in Plan B with a total of 1,350 cases and four groups in Plan A with a total of 1,800 cases.

quests, and meeting crisis situations, with only residual effort, if any, going into the initiation of additional rehabilitation and counseling services. With a work load of 250 cases, a supervisor assisted by five workers would be expected not only to administer financial assistance but also to provide an elevated level and a fuller range of other welfare services.

Because of the differing demands to be made of supervisors, differential qualifications for this position were established. It was specified that supervisors in Plan A would have bachelor's degrees only but would possess proved managerial skills; those in Plan B would have master's degrees in social work. All of the supervisors assigned to Plan A had some formal casework education in graduate schools of social work, but none had completed professional training.

There were both a "good" reason and a "real" reason for placing these "semiprofessional" supervisors with Plan A work groups. The good reason was related to the previous discussion of expected levels of service; it seemed wasteful to use a professional social worker for the limited service that seemed feasible with a caseload of 450. The real reason was that the number of professional social workers in the department—the second largest local public assistance organization in the country—was so small that to bring ten of them into the Midway office would have so depleted the number remaining as to have wreaked an immediate hardship on some of the other district offices.

| The Tooling-up Process |

The research plan provided that the duties and responsibilities of administrative and staff personnel in the Midway office would remain the same as in the other district offices. Centralized filing and other clerical services were provided only to the conventional work groups; comparable services were provided to the experimental teams by the unit clerks assigned to each team.

The six fully qualified social work supervisors were randomly assigned to experimental and conventional work groups in Plan B, and the other four supervisors were assigned in the same way to Plan A. Workers were ranked on the basis of the supervisory ratings they had received in the district offices from which they were transferred. The highest ranking thirty were randomly assigned to experimental and conventional work groups in Plan

B and the remaining twenty to Plan A. Subsequent vacancies were filled in the order in which they occurred. As soon as the cases were assigned to all workers, the research staff began to work with the supervisors and workers in the experimental groups to prepare them to operate in accordance with the team model.

It was realized, of course, that by assigning field staff to work groups randomly—and hence arbitrarily—and in changing over to the team model by fiat, heavy demands were being placed on the goodwill and cooperativeness of those assigned to experimental teams, who were forced to accept or tolerate sudden shifts from their customary responsibilities, relationships, and ways of working to ways that appeared to some of them to be less desirable. At the same time they were being asked to take on the additional burden of providing various types of research data.

A more favorable way of establishing an experimental team would have been to recruit a well-prepared casework supervisor who seemed interested in developing a team with which he could work. The supervisor might then be given a caseload of his own, perhaps forty to eighty cases. When he had become acquainted with this caseload, he would be given another caseload and two workers to assist him. The work load and staff would be increased at a pace to be regulated by the supervisor. Workers would be recruited from outside the organization, not transferred from established caseload situations. However, it was believed that the avoidance of bias required random assignment of supervisors as well as workers, and we could not afford the luxury of developing the experimental team in a gradual and relatively undemanding way.

The immediate assignment of five workers to a team supervisor meant his immediate assumption of direct responsibility for five caseloads and for making task rather than case assignments to the workers. Some of the more experienced and competent workers who were assigned to experimental teams made clear that they felt downgraded by being asked to relinquish their former caseload responsibilities to work on task assignments and under closer supervision. Within the relatively short time available, it did not seem feasible to develop staff through "job enlargement" techniques.

If we were flying in the face of certain precepts of modern management, it was because we felt impelled to place some reasonable limits on the tooling-up process and get the experiment off the ground. We acknowledged to staff the difficulty of the demands being made of them. For those assigned to Plan B the reduced caseload seemed immediately therapeutic. An important part of the effort to gain staff acceptance of the team model and to implement the changes being imposed so precipitously was to continue for some little time to help the experimental teams, and especially the team supervisors, in their new ways of working.

| Case Classification |

The research plan provided for assisting and supporting supervisors in experimental teams by supplying them with a plan for classifying cases in order of the priority of their claims. The case classification plan was designed to guide, but not determine, the supervisor's use of staff time, including his own.

The case classification for Plan B was developed on the basis of three sets of criteria: (1) presence or absence of a major social problem, (2) presence or absence of client motivation and client capacity for using service,[11] and (3) the client's degree of social vulnerability or the extent to which he constituted an immediate threat to the public safety.[12] First priority was given to clients who were in vulnerable situations or who represented threats to the public safety; second priority was given to those having the motivation and capacity to use the services that they appeared to need and that could be provided by or through the teams. Regardless of case classification, services were to be given to all clients in emergency or crisis situations. Thus while emphasis was placed on maximizing the effectiveness of available treatment resources whenever there was room for discretion, rec-

---

11. This criterion was adapted from a formulation by Lilian Ripple in *Motivation, Capacity and Opportunity: Studies in Casework Theory and Practice,* Social Service Monographs No. 3, 2d Series (Chicago: School of Social Service Administration, University of Chicago, 1964).

12. Compare Willard C. Richan, "A Theoretical Scheme for Determining Roles of Professional and Nonprofessional Personnel," *Social Work,* Vol. 6, No. 4 (October 1961), pp. 22–28. Richan used the term vulnerability in relation to possible deleterious effects of poor social services on the client; the present authors' use of the term relates to the potential threat of the environment to the client or of the client to others.

ognition was also given to the prior necessity of meeting human crises.

The assistant director of the research project instructed the experimental team supervisors in the use of the case-classification system, using both individual and group instructional methods, and assisted supervisors in the classification of the cases that were under care in the district office and that were assigned to him in a block when the teams were first organized. Thereafter the supervisor classified cases assigned to him from intake.

In addition to training in case classification, supervisors were also assisted in an initial assessment of the interests and capabilities of their workers with respect to performing different kinds of tasks in different case situations and in the technique of task assignment. Task assignments were made thereafter on the basis of the supervisor's classification of the case and his assessment of available personnel. Case classifications and personnel assessments were to be reviewed and revised periodically by supervisors in order to maintain the appropriateness of the task assignments.

The case classification plan was simplified for use by supervisors in Plan A without full professional training and with high caseload responsibilities. Cases in Plan A were classified entirely on the basis of the client's principal presenting problem. The following classification was used: (1) unmarried mothers, (2) recently deserted mothers, (3) unemployed fathers, (4) the physically handicapped, (5) the emotionally or mentally handicapped, and (6) all others, including persons in the remaining AFDC cases and nonhandicapped persons receiving Old Age Assistance.

Although implementation of the team model varied somewhat in Plan A and in Plan B, the essential elements were the same in both versions, namely, the placement with supervisors of authority and responsibility for decisions regarding service to specific clients and for direction and control of all staff resources in providing it.

| Case Assignment |

The research design called for the random assignment to work groups of cases under care at the beginning of the experiment and also those accepted subsequently. This meant that workers and teams would be responsible for cases anywhere in the district and that the traditional method of making workers responsible for all cases in a smaller geographic area within the district would be abandoned. Even staff members otherwise sympathetic to the research found this disturbing.

The first objection raised was the amount of travel involved. Workers would be obliged to criss-cross the entire district. Fortunately the researchers could point out that the district, as designed, was quite compact, and public transportation on all four borders of the district was excellent.

The second argument related to the problem of handling inquiries about who was responsible for a given client. Under the geographic assignment plan, if the client's address was known, his worker was known. In the case of district-wide (randomized) assignment, this would not be possible. Clients had to be given —and remember—their workers' names. It was in fact the case that many clients did not know their workers' names.[13] The establishment of a large wheel-type card index containing clients' names and work group assignments easily and effectively solved the problem of linking inquiring clients with responsible field staff.

After district-wide assignment had been in operation for some time, the district office staff discovered that this artifact of the experimental design had a number of advantages, not the least of which was the elimination of a large number of case transfers that would otherwise have been necessitated by clients' frequent changes of address. Now the same worker or work group could continue serving a client even if he moved within the district.

LAUNCHING THE EXPERIMENT

Experimental teams and conventional work groups were located on separate floors of the Midway District Office building. In order to emphasize their teamlike character, each experimental

---

13. This was a most useful finding to offer those staff members and others who argued against the sharing of case responsibility among team members on the grounds that it would "interfere with the casework relationship." The researchers observations were that in the department the concept of casework relationship was honored more in the breach than in the observance.

team was provided with its own partitioned office designed to accommodate the supervisor, five workers, unit clerk, and the case records and files relating to the team's work. Desks for the conventional work groups were arranged in the prevailing fashion of the other district offices: in rows on a separate open floor, with each supervisor at the end of the row accommodating his workers.

Just before the experiment was launched, caseloads were balanced out on the basis of random assignment so that each high-caseload group had approximately 450 cases and each low-caseload group, 225 cases. Cases approved at intake after the beginning of the experimental period were assigned to work groups in the ratio of one for each low-caseload work group in Plan B to two for each high-caseload group in Plan A.

Caseload turnover was high during the study period—about 27 percent a year. However, the number of assistance cases in the Midway office each month during the period of the experiment—February 1, 1963, through March 31, 1965—was quite stable, only varying between 2,796 and 3,150.

Measures of change in client behavior were to be based, not on cases already open when the experiment started, but rather on cases opened at intake in the Midway office after the beginning of the experiment, including those that had previously been opened and closed by other district offices. At the time the experiment was planned, it was estimated, on the basis of projections of the trend in the number of cases accepted at intake by the department in the previous four years, that about eight hundred cases would be acquired at intake in a twelve-month period. The sample of cases for study of client change was to consist of all cases received at intake that were served for at least one year and on which necessary information could be obtained.

At a district office staff meeting before the launching of the field experiment, the participating members of the field staff were informed of the purpose of the experiment and were assured of the confidentiality of all information given to the research staff. It was made clear that the staff were not being asked to speed up their work rate, but rather to maintain a level, "normal" work pace. Staff members were assured that the researchers would not make known to anyone—within or outside the organization—any information that could affect any staff member adversely.

The high service motivations of many of the newly recruited young workers became evident when the researchers tried to explain the concept of "present" or limited service and the modest service expectations that would be placed on staff in Plan A in view of their high caseloads. Many of the workers assigned to Plan A asked to be "permitted" to provide service at as high a level as possible. The researchers readily agreed to this, of course, and thereafter refrained from open discussion of expected levels of service from Plan A work groups.

IMPLEMENTING THE RESEARCH PLAN

Perhaps the most important difference between the research as planned and the research as conducted was the researchers' inability to gain complete acceptance of the idea of task rather than case assignment. An attempt was made to train the experimental groups in this aspect of the team form of organization during the latter part of the tooling-up period and immediately before launching the experiment, and this effort was continued during the early months of the experimental period. However, the load placed on the supervisors in accommodating to the other demands of the team model, plus resistance from some workers—especially the more senior ones—to giving up control of their caseloads, meant that task assignment was not completely achieved during the full period of the experiment in all teams in the form specified in the research plan. Nevertheless, a substantial degree of success was attained.

Circumstances that could not have been foreseen or prevented invalidated the estimates of the expected number of applications for assistance and especially for AFDC. The project's method of dealing with this is described in Chapter 4.

It was recognized that, inasmuch as both the experimental and conventional work groups were to be housed in the same office, the conventional groups might adopt aspects of the experimental model. Efforts to control such "contamination," chiefly through monitoring the activities of the supervisors of the conventional groups, appeared to be moderately successful. The effects of contamination and of anything less than complete implementation of the experimental team model would serve, of course, to diminish or blur the true differences between the operation of experimental teams and conventional groups.

| Impact of External Forces |

In addition to contamination, another problem was the impact of disturbing external forces in the environment of the experiment. A chief virtue of experimental design is that outside influences can be assumed to affect experimental and control groups in the same way and to the same extent. However, even if this is so, if outside influences are of an extremely violent nature, they may disrupt the operations of the agency in which the field experiment is being conducted or may overshadow the effects of the experimental input.

Staff members of the Midway office, along with other department staff members, were subjected to the normal misfortunes of the public assistance program, including wave after wave of administrative orders reflecting changes in federal, state, and county assistance policies. Many of these policies—such as the requirement of compulsory school attendance by adult clients—seemed to impress the field staff as being merely harassing and futile. Other administrative actions—such as a prohibition against clients having telephones or television sets and the setting of quotas for the number of cases to be closed regardless of justification—were clearly perceived as harsh and punitive. These requirements were not set by federal legislation or regulations, but were imposed by state and local authorities. Shortly after the beginning of the experiment many members of the field staff told the researchers that, reduced caseloads and new ways of working notwithstanding, in the hostile climate created by such restrictive policies they did not believe that clients would be receptive to any agency efforts to provide service. In this situation the research staff felt impelled to exercise its option to appeal for a waiver or modification in the application of these orders to the Midway office.

Fortunately, the department director had, at the researchers' request, appointed a panel of citizens to serve in an advisory capacity to the Midway Project. A number of meetings were held with this Citizen's Advisory Committee to inform them of the experiment's progress. The committee was now asked to consider the possible effects of the department's latest policies on the research. The director indicated that discretion was possible and that a review of the application of rules could be made. (When this became known to the workers in the district, many decided to exercise their own discretion immediately.)

The department director also claimed to have no knowledge of a recent communiqué that had come to the district offices from a subordinate, but authorized, official, to the effect that the job security and future advancement of all field staff would depend entirely on the number of cases closed regardless of the reasons for or the validity of the closings. This immediately evoked a strongly negative and dramatic reaction from a large number of Citizens' Advisory Committee members. The memorandum was subsequently rescinded for the department as a whole.

In the first summer of the experiment, the summer of 1963, a delay in appropriations by the state legislature, resulting from a vendetta between the two major political parties, meant that clients received no public assistance payments for more than two weeks. Later, by legislative mandate, ceilings or upper limits were imposed on the amounts allowed for clients' rent. This was especially hard on the Midway clients and field staff and thus affected the research staff, for reasons outlined in Chapter 4.

Another departmental and statewide influence that affected the field service staff was a controversy regarding the provision of birth control information and materials to public assistance recipients—a controversy that resulted in the removal by the governor of the chairman of the Illinois Public Aid Commission. Another was a threatened strike of employees because of the suspension of nine department workers who were alleged to have approved overpayments to clients. A chronic cause for festering staff resentment was a long freeze on in-grade salary increases and promotions.

Some of the costs to the organization of these adverse conditions and of a turbulent environment are reflected in the data on turnover and other measures of morale discussed in Chapter 2.

OUTLINE OF THE REPORT

The three major types of criterion measures used to measure experimental outcomes relate to (1) staff morale, (2) volume of work performed, and (3) client change. The researchers had in mind a rational-system model—that is, an organization that drew resources (e.g., money, staff, clients) from its environment and interrelated these inputs in a financial-payment and social service process designed to maximize client improvement and minimize client deterioration. Client change was therefore seen as the "payoff" criterion. However, in order to throw some light on service delivery it was decided to obtain information on how much and what kind of work the staff was doing, how staff members perceived the operation of the Midway office and the department, and how they reacted to the organization and to their roles in it.

Chiefly for purposes of structuring our own analysis, the researchers cast these measurement criteria in the following admittedly oversimplified and rather static umbrella proposition: (1) the experimental team form of organization will provide a work situation that will engender higher morale in its members than the conventional work group will, (2) therefore, the experimental teams will produce more work, (3) therefore, the clients served by experimental teams will show more positive change. In this arrangement of hypotheses, the form of work group organization was seen as the independent variable, client change as the dependent variable, and worker morale and performance as intervening variables. The costs of operating the experimental teams and the comparison or conventional work groups are considered to be approximately the same, so that the criterion of client change is taken to measure efficiency as well as effectiveness.

Worker morale will be discussed in Chapter 2, worker performance in Chapter 3, and client change in Chapter 4. Hypotheses developed for these major variables will be set forth in the chapter in which each is discussed. The connections between the hypotheses will be discussed in the concluding chapter.

Chapter Two

CHANGES IN FIELD STAFF MORALE

Staff morale—the way in which groups of employees perceive and react to their work situations—has been one of the more intensively studied aspects of organizational life. In view of the large volume of research in industry and government on manifestations of morale and the general interest of social workers in the interaction of attitudes, motivations, and human behavior, there have been remarkably few investigations of job attitudes and their correlates among social welfare workers.[1] The weight of the evidence in the general literature on formal organizations points to a negative relationship between high job satisfaction scores on the one hand and high rates of turnover and absenteeism on the other.[2]

One of the more influential descriptions of the dissatisfactions and frustrations encountered by public assistance workers was provided by Edgar May, a journalist who took employment as a fieldworker in the public welfare department of Erie County, New York, in order to write a series of newspaper articles that

1. Frederick Herzberg, Bernard Mausner, and Barbara Bloch Snyderman, *Job Attitudes: Review of Research and Opinion* (Pittsburgh: Psychological Service of Pittsburgh, 1957), contains a bibliography of more than 1,000 items. None pertains to the job attitudes of social welfare personnel.

2. Ibid., p. 105.

eventually earned him a Pulitzer Prize.[3] May criticized the haphazard system of recruiting staff and the inadequacy of their qualifications, both in technical skills and motivation. He described the continuous paperwork that occupied most of the fieldworkers' time as well as that of other staff members. Fieldworkers became intensely frustrated because clients' problems were too complicated and severe to yield to the workers' limited competence and because of the restrictive provisions of the assistance programs that impeded workers' efforts at rehabilitation.

The findings of a study of job attitudes of public assistance caseworkers and supervisors in Cook County, Illinois, conducted by Greenleigh Associates, are consistent with May's description of Erie County.[4] Levels of job satisfaction were substantially lower than those for persons in other occupations comparable in status, educational qualifications, and job requirements. Intrinsic satisfactions from performance of the public assistance job itself and its challenge and interest were moderate, and morale as a whole was lower than that generally found for professional or clerical workers in other fields. Both supervisors and workers were less satisfied with personnel policies—including pay, communications, and work organization—than their counterparts in other organizations. Supervisors consistently scored higher on all factors than their subordinates, a universal finding in job attitude studies.

Tollen's study of staff losses in public child welfare services and voluntary family agencies indicated that unsatisfactory employment conditions in public welfare contributed substantially to the high rates of turnover he discovered.[5]

These researches, along with Blau and Scott's studies of public

---

3. Edgar May, *Our Costly Dilemma* (Buffalo: *Buffalo Evening News*, 1960).

4. "Facts, Fallacies and Future: A Study of the Aid to Dependent Children Program of Cook County, Illinois" and "Addenda to Facts, Fallacies and Future" (New York: Greenleigh Associates, 1960). (Mimeographed.) The Greenleigh study is of particular interest here because it related to the Cook County Department of Public Aid, the study agency for the present research.

5. William B. Tollen, *Study of Staff Losses in Child Welfare and Family Service Agencies* (Washington, D.C.: U.S. Department of Health, Education & Welfare, Social Security Administration, Children's Bureau, 1960), pp. 109–113.

assistance organizations, provide useful background for the investigation of Midway office staff morale.[6] Blau's study agency was the general assistance office of a large city agency; Scott's was a smaller county agency. Their interest was in various aspects of the formal and informal social structures of the agency and, in particular, the ways in which work group organization affected staff behavior. These studies reveal the profound, subtle, and complex effects of the social context of the work environment on the relationships, attitudes, and roles of workers.

Among Blau and Scott's findings that influenced the Midway Project were the following: Workers were found to develop either "professional" or "bureaucratic" orientations to the job as a way of resolving the competing or contradictory requirements of the organization and the professional social work standards of some of their supervisors.[7] As compared with bureaucratic staff members, it was found that professionally oriented workers were more likely to approve increases in assistance to clients and to be less loyal to the agency. Such limited loyalty was interpreted as a consequence of the limited opportunity for career development in a public assistance agency. Workers with professional orientations were more critical of the agency than bureaucratic workers regarding discrepancies between professional values and agency practice and regarding laws, agency procedures, and agency practices that interfered with the provision of help to clients.

High cohesion in work groups was found to be effective in supporting workers at times of crisis or conflict with clients. The degree of integration of inexperienced workers with their work groups greatly influenced whether they were oriented chiefly toward providing services or toward completion of eligibility procedures.

---

6. Peter M. Blau and W. Richard Scott, *Formal Organizations: A Comparative Approach* (San Francisco: Chandler Publishing Co., 1962).

7. *See* Salomon Rettig and Benjamin Pasamanick, "Status, Work Satisfaction, and Variables of Work Satisfaction of Psychiatric Social Workers," *Mental Hygiene*, Vol. 4, No. 1 (January 1960), pp. 48–54; Irving Kermish and Frank Kuslin, "Why High Turnover? Staff Losses in a County Welfare Department," *Public Welfare*, Vol. 27, No. 2 (April 1969), pp. 134–140; and Paul E. Weinberger, "Job Satisfaction and Staff Retention in Social Work," *NASW News*, Vol. 15, No. 3 (March 1970), pp. 10, 23–24.

HYPOTHESES ON STAFF MORALE

The first and major hypothesis concerning staff morale was that members of experimental work groups will exhibit higher morale than members of conventional work groups as evidenced by (1) measures of staff attitudes, (2) rates of absenteeism, and (3) turnover rates. The second and dependent hypothesis was that these differences in morale between experimental teams and conventional work groups will be greater in Plan B, the low-caseload experiment, than in Plan A.

Although in the umbrella proposition morale was viewed as a variable mediating the influence of work organization on client change, it was assumed that the relationship between these two dependent variables was reactive. The prediction of higher morale in experimental teams was thus based in part on the hypothesis concerning superior effectiveness of the team with respect to improvement in clients. The researchers believed that supervisors and workers—whether experienced or new to the field and to the agency—would react positively to their own perceptions of the efficacy of the team form of organization. It was believed that the interaction among members of the group working jointly on cases would be a factor making for group cohesion. The provision of partitioned office space for each of the teams, placement of the supervisor in the same office as the workers, and the decentralization of clerical service and files were intended to enhance group cohesion (among workers) and hierarchical cohesion (between supervisor and worker) by providing conditions that would facilitate communication among all team members better than those provided in the conventional open-floor arrangement.[8]

In the early stages of planning, the researchers also had in mind that the team model would make possible a more rational and less traumatic induction of new workers into their duties. It was believed that this would be a major factor in supporting

---

8. The departmental formula for square footage allowance for staff and equipment was followed so that the only additional cost involved was the initial expense of shoulder-high partitions.

the morale of team members. However, in negotiating plans for organizing the Midway office, and even before the tooling-up period, it became obvious that it would be necessary to start operations with a staff consisting almost entirely of workers transferred from other districts. These workers had not only already survived their initiation into the agency, but felt highly resentful about being "downgraded." Whereas before they had been "caseworkers carrying a caseload," they were now being asked to serve as assistants to a supervising caseworker, responsible only for tasks as assigned. For staff members assigned to Plan B, the reduction of caseload tended to offset this resentment, carrying with it as it did visions of reduced paperwork and other bureaucratic requirements and increased opportunities to provide service to clients.

Tending to overshadow all of these considerations was the sharp antagonism created between the continued, intense bureaucratic emphasis of the central administrative office on enforcement of agency regulations concerning eligibility and assistance amounts and the just-as-intense desire of most of the field staff to be more effective in helping clients. Although this conflict was not unique to the Midway office, it had been exacerbated by the fact that the project had tended to attract staff members who hoped the enterprise might buffer some of the more deleterious aspects of departmental bureaucracy. However, by the time the experiment was launched, the situation seemed to have deteriorated to such an extent that the researchers were dubious about whether it would be possible to distinguish between the extremely low morale of both conventional and experimental work groups.

MEASURING STAFF MORALE

Measures of morale were obtained by means of three questionnaires. Two were quite brief and were used only with the Midway field staff. The third, and longer, questionnaire was designed for use with the total county field staff. All three instruments were administered near the beginning of the experiment in April 1963 (Time 1) and near the end of the experiment in March 1965 (Time 2).

The different work groups were organized and cases were first assigned to them in June 1962. The experimental groups began their new way of working during this period before the experiment was formally launched on February 1, 1963. The first wave of attitude schedules was administered in April 1963, so that by this time most of the staff were well acquainted with the Midway office, their job situations, and the meaning of the research project for them.

A "Staff Opinion Questionnaire on the Midway Research Project" was designed to throw light on Hawthorne and other unintentional effects that were generated during the tooling-up period. A "Staff Opinion Questionnaire on Work Organization" went directly to the matter of staff members' perceptions of and reactions to differences in work group organization. An "Employment and Job Attitude Questionnaire" was designed to obtain a comprehensive measure of employees' attitudes toward the total work situation in the work group, the district office, the department, and the public assistance field.

Hawthorne effects are those modifications of the behavior of study subjects that are attributable to factors in the research process and the study environment other than those representing intended experimental inputs. In the famous experiments of 1927–32 in the Chicago Hawthorne Works of the Western Electric Company that led to the identification of this phenomenon, it was discovered that sociopsychological satisfaction derived from participation in the experiments led to more positive work attitudes and higher production. In field experiments with human subjects it is rarely possible to eliminate Hawthorne effects, although they can be minimized in some situations through appropriate study design and execution. However, in experiments like the present one that involve training staff in new ways of working, staff attitudes toward the change process that tend to be identified by the study subjects with the research itself can easily spill over and influence work group preferences, attitudes toward the job situation as a whole, and even work behavior.

The purpose of the "Staff Opinion Questionnaire on the Midway Research Project" was to ascertain the importance of the Hawthorne effects and specifically the extent to which differences between attitudes of workers in experimental teams and in conventional work groups toward the research project itself might have influenced subsequent comparative measures of morale and work performance.

| Attitudes Toward the Research Project |

The "Staff Opinion Questionnaire on the Midway Research Project" called for responses from each member of the field staff as to whether he agreed or disagreed with the following questions:

1. The research project interferes a good deal with my work.
2. I expected that working in an office where research is going on would be more interesting than it has been.
3. Being part of a research project makes my work more important.
4. I enjoy providing information and answering questions for research staff.
5. More opportunities for informal small group discussions with the research staff are badly needed.
6. It is my impression that the research staff know what they are trying to do.
7. University control of the research program guarantees that it will be carried out effectively.
8. It is unlikely that the research program will find out anything very important.
9. We should have a much fuller explanation from research staff of what they are trying to do.

Scores representing the percentage of favorable responses (that is, agreement with positive statements or disagreement with negative statements) from field staff members in each of the four types of work groups (Plan A—Conventional and Experimental, Plan B—Conventional and Experimental) are shown in Table 1. In general the scores indicate a preponderance of unfavorable attitudes on the part of Plan A field staff and a preponderance of favorable attitudes by Plan B staff. None of the differences between the scores of the experimental and conventional work groups in Plan A or in Plan B at either Time 1 or Time 2 was

Table 1

Opinion Scores on Midway Research Project, by Type of Work Group, at Time 1 (April 1963) and Time 2 (March 1965)[a]

Type of Work Organization	Plan A Time 1	Plan A Time 2	Plan A Difference	Plan B Time 1	Plan B Time 2	Plan B Difference
Conventional work groups	49.3 (12)	47.4 (12)	—1.9	48.7 (18)	57.2 (18)	+8.5
Experimental teams	48.3 (12)	43.8 (12)	—4.5	53.8 (18)	51.8 (18)	—2.0
Difference	—1.0	—3.6	—2.6	+5.1	—5.4	—10.5

[a] Figures in parentheses represent the number of staff members included in the score.

significant at the .10 level.[9] In the subsequent presentation of job attitude scores, data for staff members who were employed throughout the experiment are shown separately from data on other staff members. Although the opinions of these "continuers" about the research were, in general, more favorable than those of other staff members, the more relevant observation for the present purpose is that, considering continuers only, there were no significant differences between the scores of conventional work groups and experimental teams in either Plan A or Plan B.

These results do not necessarily indicate that the Hawthorne effects were not operative. Indeed, the research staff, working directly with the field staff on a day-to-day basis, could hardly avoid noting expressions of affective reaction, both positive and negative, to various aspects of the research process. However, the fact that scores of staff opinion concerning the research do not differ significantly between members of experimental and conventional groups is interpreted as meaning that it is extremely

9. In the analysis of Midway staff data by type of work group, nonparametric tests were used. When the dependent variable was in the form of ordinal scales, the Mann-Whitney test was used. When changes in attitudes of individuals over time was being assessed, the Wilcoxon matched pairs sign-ranks test for related samples was used. Tests for difference of means or proportions were used for comparisons involving the total county staff of over one thousand at Time 1 and Time 2, comparisons of the total Midway staff of sixty with total community staff, or total Midway staff at Time 1 and Time 2.

Table 2

Opinion Scores on Type of Work Organization, at Time 1 (April 1963) and Time 2 (March 1965)[a]

Type of Work Organization	Plan A Time 1	Plan A Time 2	Plan A Difference	Plan B Time 1	Plan B Time 2	Plan B Difference
Conventional work groups	—38 (12)	—58 (12)	—20	80 (18)	110 (18)	+30
Experimental teams	—34 (12)	—16 (12)	+18	244 (18)	229 (18)	—15
Difference	+4	+42[b]	+38[b]	+164[b]	+119[b]	—45

[a] Figures in parentheses represent the number of staff included in the score.
[b] $p<.10$, two-tailed.

unlikely that there were differences that might disturb in any important way subsequent comparisons of reported work attitudes of members of the different types of work groups.

Work Organization Preferences

The most direct measure of staff attitudes toward different kinds of work group organization was the "Staff Opinion Questionnaire on Work Organization." All sixty members of the Midway field staff were asked to select the highest rank of each of the four types of work group organization with respect to each of thirteen work situation characteristics, ten intended as positive—such as "Provision of best quality of supervision" and "Creation of best working relationships among members of the work group"—and three intended as negative—such as "Greatest pressures of time on workers." The questionnaire provided opportunity to indicate either the highest ranking type of work group or a "no-difference" response for each question. Frequencies of highest rank assigned to positive and negative attributes provided a work organization preference score of the status ascribed by the total field staff to each type of work group with a possible range of +600 and —180. Table 2 shows aggregate preference scores based on responses from the sixty Midway office field staff members.

Of the four types of work groups, the experimental team form of organization in Plan B enjoyed the highest status by a wide margin both at the beginning and end of the experiment, apparently because it combined two changes in the organization of work that appeared to be attractive to most staff members—namely, the team approach and reduced caseload. The conventional work group in Plan B was clearly preferred over the experimental team in Plan A at both Time 1 and Time 2. This suggests that, taken alone, the caseload reduction outweighed the team form of organization in attractiveness to staff.

The general preference of public assistance field staff for low caseload assignments is perhaps the most widely known of the facts concerning public assistance staff opinion. An obvious basis for this preference is, of course, the common human resistance to work pressures that are not subject to the individual's control. This reaction is commonly defended or rationalized in the public assistance setting, as in other human service organizations, on the basis that there is an inverse relationship between quantity and quality of service provided. The implicit assumption here—an assumption that is still largely untested—is that the relationship between quantity and quality of work performed is negative and linear.

In view of the fact that thirty-six members of the field staff worked under Plan B and only twenty-four under Plan A, the preference scores would have been biased in favor of Plan B if the general tendency had been for staff members to prefer their own staff assignments. However, analysis of the relationship of work group assignment to work preference choices showed that although members of Plan B were indeed inclined to prefer their own type of group, staff assigned to Plan A tended to downgrade their groups. A tabulation of preferences, excluding those for own type of work group, gave the same substantive results as shown in Table 2, indicating that work group membership was not in itself an important determinant of comparative work group preference. This was true not only for total field staff, but also for continuers when their preferences were considered separately.

Table 2 shows that at Time 1 there was little difference in staff preference scores between Plan A conventional and experimental groups. By Time 2 the negative scores for both had increased, but more sharply for conventional work groups, so that the preference score for the experimental teams was significantly higher.

At both Time 1 and Time 2, staff preference scores for the experimental team form were significantly higher than for the conventional work group form in Plan B. The difference in change scores was not in the expected direction, but was not significant. Thus the data indicate that although caseload was more important than the organizational factor in worker preference, considering the organizational factor alone, the field staff preferred the team form to the conventional work group throughout the experiment.

| Employment and Job Attitudes |

Staff preferences concerning the organization of work groups represents those opinions most immediately and directly related to the research problem with which the Midway Project was concerned. However, in the context of the hypothesized relationship of staff morale to work output and client change, a comparison of differences in staff attitudes as a whole seems indicated.

The establishment of conventional work groups as comparison groups provided a satisfactory basis for making inferences regarding the effects of internal changes in the Midway office. However, because of the researchers' concern in the research design stage about the effect of Hawthorne factors on the Midway staff as a whole, it was deemed necessary to have some reference points external to the Midway office so that changes in attitudes arising from factors operating in the Midway office itself could be differentiated from those induced by community-wide factors and influencing the attitudes of county staff as a whole. Furthermore, it was thought useful to know the extent to which attitudes reported by staff in the conventional groups in Plan A correspond with those of the field staff in other district offices whose work group organization the conventional Plan A work groups were meant to resemble. The necessity of obtaining external reference points was pointed up by the increased uncertainties in the welfare situation in the state and county and the threats this posed for the stability of the department's operations. An agreement was reached with the department to obtain data from supervising caseworkers and workers in all district offices through an "Employment and Job Attitude Questionnaire."

The "Employment and Job Attitude Questionnaire" contained

two major sections. The first section consisted of questions pertaining to demographic, social, educational, and occupational characteristics believed to be important correlates of job attitudes. The second section, "Opinions About the Job," was designed to measure attitudes of workers and supervisors toward their work and was for the most part an adaptation of an instrument (the "Organization Survey Questionnaire") developed by the Industrial Relations Center of the University of Chicago and used widely for testing job attitudes of industrial and other employees.[10]

The "Organization Survey Questionnaire" had been standardized on a wide range of occupations, including professional staff members such as nurses, doctors, and elementary and high school teachers. Three kinds of modifications were made in adapting this instrument to the public assistance field. First, terms specific to public assistance were substituted for words that applied more appropriately to a business context. For example, "district office" or "central administrative office" were substituted for "management," "agency" was substituted for "company," and "supervisor" was substituted for "boss." A second kind of modification was the addition of several items to the inventory in order to measure attitudes toward specific aspects of the job that were peculiar to public assistance. The third and major modification was the addition of a group of items designed to measure staff attitudes about the adequacy of service provided to clients. The "Employment and Job Attitudes Questionnaire" as used at Time 2 was the same as that used at Time 1 except for necessary editorial changes.

Each item in the "Opinions About the Job" section consisted of a statement concerning some specific aspect of the job. The respondent was asked to indicate whether he agreed with, disagreed with, or was undecided about the statement in question. One-half of the items were presented in a form that expressed favorable attitudes about the job and the other half, unfavorable

---

10. David G. Moore and Richard Renck, "The Professional Employee in Industry," *Journal of Business,* Vol. 38, No. 1 (January 1965), pp. 58–66; Melany E. Baehr and Richard Renck, "The Definition and Measurement of Employee Morale," *Administrative Science Quarterly,* Vol. 3, No. 2 (September 1958), pp. 157–184.

attitudes. Agreement with a favorable statement and disagreement with an unfavorable statement were considered to be positive responses; because of the tendency to underreport unfavorable feelings in surveys of this kind and because an "undecided" response is a lukewarm endorsement at best, such a response was classed as negative.[11] All questions were given equal weight. The job attitude score for each person is the percentage of the items presented to which the subject gave a positive response.

Scores were obtained for twelve major factors of job attitudes.[12] Each factor was operationally defined by a set of six to ten items, or ninety-seven items in all. Questions were formulated to elicit an opinion about each item. The questionnaire itself did not specify the job factors, and the ninety-seven questions were arranged randomly in order to discourage respondents' perception of any classification scheme, so that each item would evoke a relatively independent response.

The population given the "Employment and Job Attitudes Questionnaire" consisted of all fieldworkers and their supervisors who were employed in all of the department's district offices on Wednesday, March 6, 1963 (Time 1), and on Wednesday, March 24, 1965 (Time 2). The questionnaire was administered simultaneously by members of the research staff to workers assembled in their own district office during office time, and assurances were given of the confidentiality of responses.

The study population for Time 1 was 1,052. Of this number, 1,002 usable questionnaires were returned for a completion rate of 95.2 percent. The study population at Time 2 was 1,089, and 1,052 usable questionnaires were returned for a completion rate of 96.6 percent.

In the results of the job attitude study, scores for supervisors were combined with scores for workers. In general supervisors' scores were higher than those of workers. However, as it turned out, there were no significant differences between scores of experimental or conventional work groups in the Midway office, regardless of whether supervisors' scores were included.

---

11. Nigel Walker, *Morale in the Civil Service: A Study of the Desk Worker* (Edinburgh, Scotland: Edinburgh University Press, 1961), p. 151.

12. These factors are shown in Table 5, p. 46.

JOB ATTITUDE SCORES OF COUNTY FIELD STAFF | A comparison of the average job attitude scores for staff in the Midway office with those of other district offices is shown in Table 3.

Data for continuers provide comparisons of attitudes of the same people at different times. These are staff members having the maximum, and hence the same, period of exposure to the experimental situation. Their responses provide the most unequivocal and sensitive data available from the job attitude study for comparisons of changes in morale for members of the different types of work group.

Table 3

Job Attitude Scores of Midway and Other Field Staff at Time 1 (April 1963) and Time 2 (March 1965)[a]

Staff	Time 1	Time 2	Difference
All field staff			
Other district offices	57.8 (955)	49.7 (1,002)	—8.1[b]
Midway office	57.3 (60)	56.5 (60)	—0.8
Difference	—0.5	+6.8[b]	+7.3
Continuers[c]			
Other district offices	60.6 (380)	51.2 (380)	—9.4[b]
Midway office	64.6 (27)	57.7 (27)	—6.9
Difference	+4.0[b]	+6.5[b]	+2.5
Other staff[d]			
Other district offices	56.0 (575)	48.7 (622)	—7.3[b]
Midway office	51.3 (33)	55.6 (33)	+4.3
Difference	—4.7[b]	+6.9[b]	+11.6

[a] Figures in parentheses are the number of staff members represented by that score. A plus sign indicates a difference in the expected direction; a minus sign indicates a difference in the opposite direction.

[b] $p<.10$.

[c] For the Midway office, the scores for continuers include all field staff who were employed in this office from Time 1 to Time 2. For other district offices, the scores for continuers include all field staff who were employed in any district office from Time 1 to Time 2—a somewhat more inclusive definition. This difference in definition does not, however, substantively affect the comparisons shown here.

[d] Scores at Time 1 are for early leavers; scores at Time 2 are for late arrivers.

Comparison of data for other staff—that is, early leavers and late arrivers—shows differences in attitudes between different populations at different points in time. However, both populations had some exposure to the experimental situation and, of special importance, were exposed to the attitudes and behavior of the continuers in their respective work groups. The contagion of attitudes among members of work groups is, of course, a most important aspect of the dynamics of staff attitude formation in any organization. In an agency characterized by high turnover it is especially important in assessing changes in organizational morale to obtain data on attitudes of all employees in the study and to examine the interaction of all the important populations making up the total staff. The only field office staff employees not included in the job attitude study were those who arrived after Time 1 and left before Time 2.

The social characteristics of the continuers in both the Midway and other district offices were significantly different from those of other staff members in a number of attributes that were found to be positively related to job attitude scores. As a result, the scores of the continuers, both in the Midway office and in other district offices, were consistently higher than those of other staff members. The continuers in both the Midway and the other district offices were more likely than other staff members to be black women, over 30, married, in supervisory positions, having more than three years' employment with the department, and having some social work education. As a result of widespread discrimination against blacks, including black women, for white-collar employment in business and industry, the department offered to this population, most of whom were college graduates but who had not completed their professional social work education, positions promising relatively high status, salary, security, and opportunity for further education and advancement. (The most common alternative employment seemed to be as teachers in a public school system.)

At Time 1, there was little difference between the job attitude scores of the Midway office staff and those of the combined field staffs in all other district offices. Although important Hawthorne and other unintended effects associated with the establishment of the Midway office and the launching of the field experiment may have been present at this time, their effects on job attitudes nevertheless seemed to have been rather evenly balanced. This finding parallels the results of the analysis of staff preferences regarding type of work group.

Two years later at Time 2, morale was significantly higher in the Midway office than in the other district offices. This was not the result of an improvement in morale among Midway field staff —the job attitude score for all field staff in the Midway office was about the same at the end as at the beginning of the experiment—but rather because of the significant deterioration of morale in the other district offices.

The score for continuers dropped significantly from Time 1 to Time 2 for the other district office staff. A smaller decline in the Midway office was offset by a small rise in the scores for other staff, whereas in the other district offices late arrivers had a lower score at Time 2 than early leavers had shown at Time 1. It could be expected from other studies of changing job attitudes that the attitudes of continuers would become somewhat more positive during the two years of the experiment and that new staff members would hold relatively high positive attitudes during the early months of employment, followed by a sharp drop and then a gradual rise.[13] The net effect of these trends for the two classes of employees, in the absence of important organizational change or accelerated turnover, would be to maintain job attitudes at a more or less constant level. The relatively low score of 48.7 for late arrivers in the other district offices thus portended a continuing decline in staff morale. In the spring of 1966, one year after the Time 2 study, this decline in staff morale was expressed in the first strike in the history of the State of Illinois against a public welfare agency, which was conducted by employees of the Cook County Department of Public Aid.

If the field staff in the Midway office had varied significantly from the staff in the other district offices with respect to social

13. R. L. Hull and Arthur Kolsted, "Morale on the Job," in Goodwin Watson, ed., *Civilian Morale* (Boston: Houghton Mifflin Co., 1942); H. Y. C. McClusky and Floyd J. Strayer, "Reactions of Teachers to the Teaching Situation—A Study of Job Satisfaction," *School Review*, Vol. 48, No. 7 (October 1940), pp. 612–623.

characteristics that were correlated with job attitude scores, comparisons between the two might have been biased by these differences. Using county-wide data on the relation of staff characteristics to job attitudes, a series of weights or correction factors were developed and first applied to the data shown in Table 3 (page 39). However, this standardizing procedure resulted in data that did not produce any significant changes in the comparisons shown in that table.

Although Midway field staff were randomly assigned to experimental and conventional work groups, because of the small number of staff members involved it was not possible to distribute staff equally among the different types of work groups according to characteristics correlated with job attitudes. However, application of weights developed from the county-wide data to the scores of experimental teams and conventional work groups in the Midway office given in Table 4 again resulted in no substantive change in the comparisons shown in that table.

The work situation structured for the conventional work groups in Plan A was intended to be similar to that of the work group organization in the other district offices. A comparison of the job attitude scores shown in Table 4 of 55.6 at Time 1 and 49.1 at Time 2 for the relatively few persons (twelve) in conventional work groups in the Midway office with the scores shown in Table 3 of 57.8 at Time 1 and 49.7 at Time 2 for the approximately one thousand persons in the other district offices reveals a rather remarkable correspondence. This close correspondence was interpreted as an encouraging indication of the validity of considering the conventional work groups in the Midway office as exemplars or prototypes of work groups in the department as a whole and also as providing evidence of the rather neutral or balanced Hawthorne effect of the Midway research operation on Midway office job attitude scores.

JOB ATTITUDE SCORES BY TYPE OF WORK GROUP | The data for all field staff in Plans A and B are characterized by similarities in the scores for the different types of work groups at Time 1 and their stability between Time 1 and Time 2. None of the differences between the scores of conventional and experimental groups is statistically significant.

Nevertheless the data for Plan A suggest that the team form of organization may have been sufficiently supportive of staff morale to offset the generally negative influences operating throughout the county and in the conventional high-caseload groups. The Plan A data for all field staff, for example, show almost no change (+0.4) from Time 1 to Time 2 in the job attitude scores of staff in the experimental teams, while the scores for the conventional work groups declined (—6.5 points). The data for both continuers and other staff members show the same

Table 4

Job Attitude Scores of Midway Field Staff, by Plan and Type of Work Group, Time 1 (April 1963) and Time 2 (March 1965)[a]

Type of Work Organization	Plan A			Plan B		
	Time 1	Time 2	Difference	Time 1	Time 2	Difference
All field staff						
Conventional	55.6	49.1	—6.5	57.2	59.3	+2.1
work groups	(12)	(12)		(18)	(18)	
Experimental	54.9	55.3	+0.4	60.1	59.5	—0.6
teams	(12)	(12)		(18)	(18)	
Difference	—0.7	+6.2	+6.9	+2.9	+0.2	—2.7
Continuers						
Conventional	56.4	48.2	—8.2	74.5	60.8	—13.7[b]
work groups	(4)	(4)		(8)	(8)	
Experimental	58.1	58.6	+0.5	63.2	58.6	—4.6
teams	(5)	(5)		(10)	(10)	
Difference	+1.7	+10.4	+8.7	—11.3[b]	—2.2	+9.1
Other Staff[c]						
Conventional	55.2	49.6	—5.6	43.3	58.0	+14.7[b]
work groups	(8)	(8)		(10)	(10)	
Experimental	52.6	53.0	+0.4	56.3	60.7	+4.4
teams	(7)	(7)		(8)	(8)	
Difference	—2.6	+3.4	+6.0	+13.0[b]	+2.7	—11.3

[a] Figures in parentheses are the number of staff members represented by that score.

[b] $p < .10$.

[c] Scores at Time 1 are for early leavers; scores at Time 2 are for late arrivers.

profile of almost no change in the scores of experimental teams and decreases in the scores for conventional work groups.

Unlike the results for Plan A, the changes from Time 1 to Time 2 in the scores for both conventional work groups and experimental teams in Plan B represent a balancing-out between continuers and other staff members of changes in opposing directions. A significant decrease from Time 1 to Time 2 of 13.7 in the scores of continuers in conventional work groups was more than offset by a significant increase of 14.7 for other staff in conventional work groups. An explanation for these changes in opposite directions within the same type of work group must be sought in the differential effects of the caseload reduction factor on staff attitudes.

Observations of the field staff suggest the following ad hoc explanation. The granting of reduced caseloads was generally accompanied by incorporation by the staff members in Plan B of the research staff's formally expressed expectation that increased and more effective service would be provided to clients. The short-range effect of reduced caseloads produced an unmistakable upward surge in morale. However, the more conscientious and sensitive workers perceived—some sooner than others—that they did not possess the necessary professional skills or developed capacities to meet successfully the challenge posed by the opportunity to provide extended and improved service. The contradictions inherent in official department behavior with respect to the withholding of financial assistance while at the same time verbally offering other social services, and the other numerous discrepancies between publicly stated policy and administrative practice, created confusion and despair for many members of the Midway staff, but especially for those in Plan B on whom the expectation of improved service had been placed.

The dilemma in which the field staff in conventional work groups in Plan B found themselves produced widely divergent reactions. Those who continued through the experiment had a Time 1 score of 74.5, the highest shown (see Table 4, page 43). At the same time those who were more immediately and profoundly discouraged and who left before the end of the experiment had a score of 43.3, the lowest shown (see Table 4). The job attitudes of persons leaving an organization generally tend to be lower than those of persons remaining, and this proved to be the case for all four types of work organization, but the difference just noted at Time 1 between the continuers and the early leavers in the Plan B conventional work groups is extreme. By Time 2 the score of the continuers in the Plan B conventional work groups had dropped to 60.8. The late arrivers in these work groups had apparently assimilated the attitudes of the continuers. They came up with a similar score of 58.0.

The Plan B experimental team staff, who had been exposed to the same pushes and pulls involved in caseload reduction as staff in Plan B conventional work groups, showed a more stable pattern of job attitude response, which is ascribed to the modifying effects of factors associated with the team form of organization. Additional work demands placed on experimental teams in connection with the research process—such as the changeover from case to task assignment and the necessity to learn and apply a somewthat sophisticated plan of case classification (considerably more complex than that required of the experimental teams in Plan A)—that were begun in the tooling-up period were still burdensome at Time 1 and seemed to offset the immediate positive reactions to reduced caseloads. In the long run and with continued exposure to the experimental input, the supportive aspects of the team form of organization served to limit the drop in the scores of the continuers in the experimental teams from Time 1 to Time 2 to 4.6, as compared with a decline of 13.7 for the conventional work groups.

MAJOR JOB COMPONENTS | The scores for the Midway field staff for each of the major job factors at Time 1 are shown in Table 5. At Time 1 the following significant differences were found among the different types of work group organization in the major factor scores for all Midway staff members:

1. Members of experimental teams in Plan A had more positive attitudes toward immediate supervision than their counterparts in the conventional work groups.

2. Members of experimental teams in Plan B had more positive attitudes toward their work associates than their counterparts in the conventional work groups.

3. Conventional work groups in Plan A had more positive attitudes toward general work organization than their counterparts in experimental teams. The term "work organization" in-

Table 5

Opinions About the Job Scores of Midway Office Field Staff, by Type of Work Group, Time 1 (April 1963) (percentage)

	Plan A			Plan B		
Job Factors[a]	Conventional	Experimental	Difference	Conventional	Experimental	Difference
Administrative effectiveness (7)	53.6	55.9	+2.3	57.9	58.7	+0.8
Client services (10)	56.7	41.7	—15.0	58.3	44.4	—13.9
Communication effectiveness (10)	55.0	60.0	+5.0	51.1	57.2	+6.1
Immediate supervision (9)	53.7	75.0	+21.3[b]	70.4	79.6	+9.2
Job satisfaction (6)	76.4	72.2	—4.2	75.0	79.6	+4.6
Organization identification (7)	50.0	50.0	00.0	50.8	60.3	+9.5
Pay and benefits (8)	33.3	19.8	—13.5	29.1	25.0	—4.1
Personnel development (6)	45.8	55.6	+9.8	49.1	56.5	+7.4
Supervisory practices (10)	54.2	65.0	+10.8	70.0	80.0	+10.0
Work associates (6)	66.7	73.6	+6.9	64.8	78.7	+13.9[b]
Work efficiency (10)	57.5	50.0	—7.5	49.4	53.3	+3.9
Work organization (8)	69.8	44.8	—25.0[b]	59.7	59.0	—0.7
Total (97)	55.6	54.9	—0.7	57.2	60.1	+2.9

[a] The number of items is shown in parentheses after each job factor.

[b] $p<.05$, two-tailed.

cludes the organization of the district office and the department as a whole and hence its meaning is broader than the term "work group organization."

At Time 2 there were no significant differences between experimental and conventional work groups in either Plan A or B in any job factor. Of the ninety-seven items in the "Opinions About the Job" section of the "Employment and Job Attitudes Questionnaire," fewer than one-third were worded to evoke responses that relate exclusively to work group factors. Consequently the impact of the experimental input would have had to be quite great to result in significantly different changes in attitude scores between experimental and conventional work groups in either of the two plans, and the data do not show that such changes occurred.

However, the supportive effect on staff morale of the team form of organization on specific factors in morale becomes visible when scores for continuers only are considered and when the difficulty encountered in determining significant differences because of the relatively small number of workers assigned to each of the four types of work groups is met by combining the data for Plans A and B.[14] A comparison of the combined continuer scores for experimental teams in Plans A and B with the combined scores for conventional work groups in the two plans is shown in Table 6. For conventional work groups, total job attitude scores decreased significantly from Time 1 to Time 2, and all twelve components of the job attitude scores decreased—seven of them significantly. The job attitude scores of continuers in experimental teams did not decline significantly, and changes in the components of their scores showed a mixed picture.

The only major job component to show a significant decrease for continuers in both the combined conventional work groups and the combined experimental teams was immediate supervision. The detailed responses from workers on the job attitude study indicated that complaints were most frequent about super-

14. The work situations in Plans A and B differ in a number of respects but have enough in common to lend some validity to the combining of their results in the way described here.

Table 6

Opinions About the Job Scores of Continuers, for Experimental and Conventional Work Groups in Plans A and B Combined, Time 1 (April 1963) and Time 2 (March 1965) (percentage)

Job Factors[a]	Experimental Teams			Conventional Work Groups		
	Time 1	Time 2	Difference	Time 1	Time 2	Difference
Administrative effectiveness (7)	63.8	55.2	—8.6	69.0	58.3	—11.7
Client services (10)	47.3	54.7	10.2[b]	67.5	62.5	—5.0
Communication effectiveness (10)	60.7	57.3	—3.4	72.5	57.5	—15.0[b]
Immediate supervision (9)	78.5	65.2	—13.3[b]	79.6	62.9	—16.7[b]
Job satisfaction (6)	86.7	78.9	—7.8	83.3	66.7	—16.6[b]
Organization identification (7)	59.0	49.5	—9.5	74.3	46.6	—17.9[b]
Pay and benefits (8)	29.2	32.5	3.3	28.1	25.0	—3.1
Personnel development (6)	55.6	50.0	—5.6	63.8	45.8	—18.0[b]
Supervisory practices (10)	79.3	73.3	—6.0	80.8	68.3	—12.5[b]
Work associates (6)	78.9	77.8	—1.1	83.3	69.4	—13.9
Work efficiency (10)	52.7	61.3	8.6	69.1	55.0	—14.1[b]
Work organization (8)	55.0	50.0	—5.0	76.0	64.5	—11.5
Total (97)	61.5	58.6	—2.9	68.5	56.6	—11.9[c]

[a] The number of items is shown in parentheses after each job factor.

[b] $p<.10$.

[c] $p<.05$.

visors' failure to give credit for good work, to encourage initiative or new ideas, and to be decisive. Direct observations of staff behavior suggest that the decline in the job component of immediate supervision reflects the tendency of many workers to project and focus their general dissatisfaction with the work situation on the closest authority figure. These observations do not suggest that the range of differences in attitudes of experimental and conventional work group members can be attributed to the idiosyncratic characteristics of supervisors.

Even in the face of the generalized dissatisfaction with immediate supervision, the general supportive effects of the team form of organization can be seen in the facts that (1) the decline in the total score of the combined experimental teams from Time 1 to Time 2 was less than that for combined conventional work groups and (2) the declines for each of the nine components that did show decreases were less than those reported by conventional work groups and only one was significant. Moreover, the combined experimental teams reported increases for three job components and the increase for a crucial one—client services—was statistically significant.

The data shown in Table 6 and the details behind them suggest that the team form of organization afforded better feedback and more frequent interaction among peers than the conventional work group and thus—despite the emphasis in the formal structure of the experimental teams on increasing the level of supervisory authority and responsibility—the decreased dependency of workers on supervisors for information about achievement. A special study of peer-group communication among Midway staff members confirmed the conclusion that the team form of organization encouraged lateral communication among members of the experimental teams.[15]

In view of the severe pathology prevalent in the public assistance population and the lack of professional education and the limited skill of many of the fieldworkers, the impact of clients'

---

15. Claire M. Anderson, "Work Group Communication Among Welfare Workers," pp. 97–98. Unpublished Ph.D. dissertation, University of Chicago, School of Social Service Administration, 1966.

problems on staff was likely to be severe and to result in intense feelings of frustration, inadequacy, and failure. In the experimental teams the impact of clients' pathology on workers—especially the younger, less experienced ones—could be absorbed better because responsibility for treatment of cases remained with the supervisors and because of the formally structured expectation that supervisors would take the initiative and intervene directly in situations that were observed to be overwhelming for workers.

STAFF ABSENTEEISM AND TURNOVER

The official records of the department were used to obtain data on absences and separations. The use of absenteeism as a measure of morale is based on the idea that some absences from work represent a form of withdrawal from distasteful, too difficult, or otherwise unsatisfactory work situations and that such withdrawal is an important enough factor in total labor force absenteeism to produce an inverse relationship between absence rates and level of morale.

The term absence as used here means time for which a staff member was paid without his being present for work. It thus includes tardiness, unexcused leave, and all excused leave with pay—sick leave, educational leave, and leave for vacation. The various forms of absenteeism do not, of course, have the same connotations for morale. Educational leave, for example, may indicate a positive rather than negative attitude toward the organization, and other forms of leave may be unrelated to or quite neutral in relation to morale. Nevertheless, the most comprehensive definition of absence is used here because of the difficulty in establishing reasons for not being at work, inasmuch as staff members could use different kinds of leave interchangeably.

All district office employees were subject to the department's requirement that they sign in and out on time sheets, which were under the control of the district office manager. Absenteeism rates, obtained by dividing the total amount of time that Midway staff members were absent from work by the amount of time on

Table 7

Absenteeism Rates in the Midway Office, February 1, 1963—March 31, 1965, by Continuers and Other Field Staff and Type of Work Group, Plan A and Plan B [a]

Type of Work Group	Plan A	Plan B
All field staff		
Conventional work groups	15.4 (31)	14.7 (34)
Experimental teams	13.5 (26)	14.7 (38)
Difference	+1.9	0.0
Continuers		
Conventional work groups	14.8 (4)	12.4 (8)
Experimental teams	13.6 (5)	13.9 (10)
Difference	+1.2	—1.5
Other staff		
Conventional work groups	15.8 (27)	16.6 (26)
Experimental teams	13.5 (21)	15.8 (28)
Difference	+2.3	+0.8

[a] Figures in parentheses are the number of staff members represented by that rate.

the payroll during the period of the experiment, are shown in Table 7.

The absenteeism rates for the experimental teams in Plan A were lower than those for conventional work groups for both continuers and other staff. The results of Plan B comparisons are mixed; the rates for continuers in experimental teams were higher than for continuers in the conventional work groups, but lower for other staff and the same for all staff.

The final measure of staff morale used was separation from employment, or rate of turnover. Data on separations, like those on absences, provide fairly objective indicators of staff morale. The rationale for their use for this purpose and for adopting the most comprehensive definition parallels that outlined for the use of absenteeism data. It should be noted that the separation of an individual from an organization is not necessarily dysfunc-

Table 8

Gross and Net Turnover Rates for Field Staff in the Midway Office, February 1, 1963—March 31, 1965 [a]

Type of Work Organization	Plan A		Plan B	
	Gross	Net	Gross	Net
Conventional work groups	145.3	119.7	90.4	90.4
Experimental Teams	101.7	93.2	114.3	85.7
Difference	+43.6	+26.5	—23.9	+4.7

[a] Rates are expressed as number of persons separated per hundred persons employed. The number of persons employed is the mean of the number on the payroll at the end of each month of the experimental period.

tional for the individual or the organization. However, the use of turnover rates as an indicator of morale is based on the assumption that in general the rate of turnover is inversely related to the level of staff morale.

One of the standard procedures for computing turnover rates—and the one adopted here—is to divide the number of separations from the organization during a given period by the average number of employees during that same period. The researchers were interested in the rate of separation from the different types of work groups as well as from the department. Turnover rates based on all separations of Midway field staff from their work groups, including transfer of staff to other positions in the Midway office and elsewhere in the department, are shown in Table 8 as gross turnover rates. Rates based on all separations of Midway field staff from the department are shown as net turnover rates.

Based on gross rates, turnover in experimental teams was lower than for conventional work groups in Plan A and higher in Plan B. Based on net rates, turnover in experimental teams was lower than in conventional work groups in both plans.

SUMMARY

Data were obtained for the following measures of morale: (1) work group preferences, (2) employment and job attitude, (3) absenteeism rates, and (4) turnover rates, gross and net.

1. Work group preference scores provide a subjective but direct and sharply focused comparison of the attractiveness for field staff of the conventional form of work group organization with the conventional form under conditions of both high and low caseload.

2. Employment and job attitude scores provide a comparison of the effects of differences in work group organization on the attitudes of field staff toward their total job situations—including not only the perception and reaction of each staff member to the performance of his own work group but also the operation of the district office, the department, and the public assistance program as a whole. This measure was therefore not only subjective in nature but most comprehensive in coverage and consequently less sensitive than the work preference measure to the effects of differences in group organization alone. Nevertheless, because job attitude scores are the most comprehensive measure of morale that is amenable to testing for significance of differences, it becomes the critical measure for testing the hypothesis concerning morale.

3. Absenteeism and turnover rates are more objectively based than are the employment and job attitude scores but are likely to be influenced by an equally wide range of personal and social factors.

Most of the measures used ranked the morale of the various types of work groups from highest to lowest as follows: (1) Plan B experimental teams, (2) Plan B conventional work groups, (3) Plan A experimental teams, (4) Plan A conventional work groups. The results of the comparisons made in Tables 2–8 between morale measures for conventional work groups and experimental teams are given in Table 9.

Inasmuch as none of the differences between experimental and conventional work group job attitude scores for all Midway staff (Table 4, page 43) is statistically significant and since the various other measures used are not amenable to statistical treatment as a combined body of data, the hypotheses concerning morale are not supported. However, the consistency of the positive direction of the results for Plan A, total staff and continuers, cannot be ignored, and the data strongly suggest that the team form of organization did have a favorable effect on the morale of team members in the high-caseload situation.

The results for Plan B are quite equivocal and reflect the confounding effects of the caseload reduction factor. The results for continuers are more positive than for the staff as a whole, suggesting at least that with the passage of time and sustained exposure, the morale of the staff in the experimental teams in Plan B was favorably influenced by the experimental input.

The researchers' view of the implication of these findings for the present research and for administrative practice is as follows: The findings do not support the idea that adoption of the team form of organization alone is likely to be an effective means of improving staff morale in an organization whose operation is generally dysfunctional for meeting the needs of its staff. On the other hand, if there are other compelling or even satisfactory rea-

Table 9

Relation of Various Measures of Morale to the Major Hypothesis on Staff Morale [a]

Measure	Combined Plans		Plan A		Plan B	
	Total staff	Continuers	Total staff	Continuers	Total staff	Continuers
Work group preference score	—	+	+	+	—	+
Job attitude score	+	+	+	+	—	+
Rate of absence	+	—	+	+	—	—
Rate of turnover, gross	+	[b]	+	[b]	—	[b]
Rate of turnover, net	+	[b]	+	[b]	+	[b]

[a] A plus sign is shown for each difference that is in the direction of the hypothesis that members of experimental teams will show higher morale than members of conventional work groups, and a minus sign for each difference that does not go in the direction of this hypothesis.

[b] The nature of the turnover measure does not permit the separation of rates for continuers from other staff members.

sons for adopting the team form of work group organization, the data provide no grounds for concern that the benefits to be derived would be tempered or offset by any possible negative effects on staff morale. Indeed, the data indicate that in organizational situations similar to that in which this experiment was conducted, the chances of supportive effects on morale would be greater than the chances of deleterious effects. The researchers' experience in instituting the team form of organization under time-limited project conditions leads us to believe that the likelihood of obtaining desired results through the team form of organization would be greatly enhanced if the experimental teams were staffed with recruits new to the organization or, failing that, through a more gradual changeover process that would provide an opportunity for participation of field staff members in decisions regarding their ways of working.

Analysis of the data on performance of work groups in Chapter 3 and changes in families and individuals proceeds on the basis of the finding that the major and dependent hypotheses concerning the positive effects of the team form of organization are not supported.

Chapter Three

CHANGES IN WORK PERFORMANCE

The general hypotheses covering work performance were similar in form to those for staff morale and were as follows: (1) The experimental teams will perform more work than the conventional work groups. (2) The superiority in the volume of work performed by the experimental team will be greater in the Plan B situation than in Plan A.

Organizational inputs of field staff can be related to outputs and to outcomes through the use of a hierarchy of interrelated measurement units ranging from the staff activity representing the most elementary and recognizable form of the work input of a social welfare worker to the end product or ultimate outcome, such as client rehabilitation.[1] Work measurement procedures provide a framework for the making of test comparisons on the volume of work performed by experimental teams and conventional work groups.

The work measurement procedure used here was developed for

1. Claire M. Anderson, Edward E. Schwartz, and Narayan Vishwanathan, "Approaches to the Analysis of Social Service Systems," in Edward E. Schwartz, ed., *PPBS and Social Welfare* (Chicago: School of Social Service Administration, University of Chicago, 1970), pp. 42–51.

the child welfare field and later applied to a statewide public welfare department, including the public assistance program.[2] As adapted for use in the Midway Project, only two levels of measurement were used, namely, the primary count—the *activity unit*—and a secondary or derived measure—the *work unit,* which in this report is also termed the *service unit.*

DATA COLLECTION

The collection of work measurement data began with the recording by field staff of their activities. The activities of public assistance field staff can be classified as (1) those involving direct contact with clients and their families and other persons in the client system, (2) activities closely related to client contacts and identifiable with specific cases such as travel to clients' homes and recording of contacts, and (3) those more remotely related to client contacts, such as general supervision and other administrative duties.

It has generally been assumed by those persons primarily interested in the administration of financial assistance and also by those primarily interested in the provision of other welfare services that direct contact with clients in the form of interviews, whether for investigation or counseling, represents the critical activity of field staff. A corollary assumption is that the more interviews, the better. This is usually stated more flatly in the public assistance field than in some other areas of social welfare, possibly because the characteristically large public assistance caseload means that too frequent contact is not seen as a present danger. For these reasons, and also because of the relative ease

2. Edward E. Schwartz, "Adoption and Foster Home Costs," in Schwartz and Martin Wolins, *Cost Analysis in Child Welfare Services,* Children's Bureau Publication No. 366 (Washington, D.C.: U.S. Government Printing Office, 1958); and *Cost Analysis and Performance Budgeting in Child Welfare and Public Assistance, State Of Maine* (New York: Laurin Hyde & Associates, 1962).

in data collection, interview counts have traditionally been used in describing staff effort or work performed in social agencies providing services to individuals and families. In the Cook County Department of Public Aid, efforts to increase interviewing activity—and especially home visiting—took the form of a specification that each worker should spend an average of three days of each workweek in the field. The chief reason for encouraging this kind of activity was to increase the frequency of checks on the client's eligibility and on the amount of financial aid for which he was currently eligible.

Although interview counts are useful in describing discrete staff efforts, it is difficult to relate these counts to the service delivered to clients. A worker visiting a client with a specific interview aim in mind may, on the basis of new information received in the course of the interview, shift the focus of his work. Moreover, the completion of a task usually requires more than one interview and sometimes interviews with more than one person. The work unit represents an effort to provide an additional dimension to the measure of staff work and especially to assist in the transition from a description of staff effort to a description of services delivered to clients. The work or service unit, as used in this research, consists of an interview or a series of immediately related interviews by a field staff member directed to a designated problem of a client or his family. The service unit thus combines a prospective and retrospective view of a task or episode of service, whether assigned to a worker by a supervisor or performed by the supervisor himself.[3]

A daily log or journal form that was required of all field staff by the department was modified to serve as a basis of the Midway office work measurement system. In addition to home visits with clients and other field interviews reported by fieldworkers in all district offices of the department, telephone interviews were reported if in the opinion of the worker they were of substantial import for the the treatment of the client. This information was collected on the suggestion of the Midway field staff, who felt that a significant part of their work was conducted over the telephone. Each interview was described in terms of (1) its major aim, (2)

3. *See* the discussion of task, pp. 12–13.

the type of interview, (3) the relationship of the interviewee to the grantee, and (4) the category of assistance provided to the client.

Field staff reported work units on a service summary form specifically designed for this purpose. In addition to identifying data on client and worker, the service summary contained data describing the origin of service and the completed service. Each service summary represented one or more interviews conducted by a worker and a service provided. The initiation and completion of each service summary were reported by the worker providing the service. Data on all the daily interview reports relating to a given service summary were electronically collated by case number to control and supplement the service summaries prepared by each field staff member.

| Problems in the Reporting of Data |

To field staff, reporting on the service summary form represented a burden in addition to the paperwork already required by the department. The research staff invested considerable time and effort in instructing field staff in the purpose of the work measurement system and the use of the service summary form, and the form itself was simplified after a short experience with it. Nevertheless, field staff continued to find this reporting burdensome, and it became to them the most objectionable aspect of the entire research project.

In general the reliability of the data obtained in this experiment appears to be in inverse relationship to the effort required of the field staff. The most reliable data are those for client change, which were produced entirely by the research staff. The least reliable data are those on work measurement, which required continuous reporting by the field staff. Data on worker morale fall in an intermediate position.

Use of the service summary form required not only continuous reporting but also an understanding of and an ability to use the concept behind the entire procedure—namely, that the provision of social service involves a purposive problem-solving process. This was a novel idea for many members of the field staff, and they had difficulty in identifying, in specific situations, the client's need or problem on which they were working and the relationship of their own activities to that problem.

The service unit concept—and indeed the work measurement system as a whole—were designed to be consonant with the problem-solving responsibility included in and characterizing the duties of experimental team supervisors. There was therefore no question about the desirability or propriety of instructing them and other team members as to the conceptual base and the proper use of service summary reporting. However, work along the same lines was begun with conventional work groups with some concern that exposing them to "problem-solving stimuli" might result in some contamination or at least dilution of their differences from the experimental teams. The researchers were soon reassured on this score when we saw how well defended most of the field staff were against changing their ways of working.

Interview Reporting

Interview reporting through a simple daily log or journal, once well established, usually involves relatively little continuing resistance or resentment on the part of field staff. However, in the Midway Project these data were used to control the service summary reporting, and field staff soon became aware that complete reporting of interviews served to alert the research staff to incomplete reporting on service summaries. To avoid the more onerous service summary reporting, some workers attempted to avoid the simple reporting required by the daily log or journal. As a consequence it must be accepted that the work measurement data were in general underreported and cannot be taken as a measure of the total volume of work performed. This is a limitation on the descriptive and other incidental use of data. However, the essential use of the data here is to compare the performance of the experimental teams and conventional work groups, and no systematic bias was detected in the reporting of work performed of a kind that would affect this use of the data.

Data on interviews are available from the beginning of the project in February 1963 to its completion in March 1965. The more complex reporting of service units was not, however, effective until September 1963. The discussion that follows, which includes analysis of activity and service units, is therefore based on data for the nineteen-month period September 1963–March 1965 and for all field staff, including both supervisors and workers.

TIME GIVEN TO INTERVIEWING | In the nineteen-month reporting period the field staff reported 46,769 interviews. The proportion of field staff time given to interviewing was determined through time studies conducted on selected days during the months of October and November 1963 and during a comparable period in 1964.[4] The relative importance of interviewing activity to the total disposition of authorized time, as represented by sixty staff positions (including vacant ones), estimated on the basis of the time study data is as follows: time authorized, 100 percent; vacancies, 4 percent; absences, 15 percent; interview time reported, 17 percent; other time, 64 percent.

If time paid for (time authorized less time not used because of staff vacancies) is used as the base, interview time reported becomes 18 percent. If work time reportable (time paid for less allowed vacations and other excused time) is the base, interview time reported becomes 21 percent.

These estimates are based on the performance of total field staff including supervisors. Supervisors, of course, had responsibilities in addition to service provision; therefore a smaller proportion of their work involved direct contact with clients. Although supervisors represented 16 percent of the total field staff, they were responsible for only 6 percent of all interviews reported. If supervisory activity is excluded, the estimated proportion of time that was reported as being devoted to interviewing would be increased to 23 percent of reportable time.[5]

Interviewing activities include not only telephone, office, and

4. *See* Hirobumi Uno, "Work Patterns of Work Groups in the Administration of Public Assistance." Unpublished Ph.D. dissertation, School of Social Service Administration, University of Chicago, 1966.

5. A previous time study using the same method showed that 25 percent of the reportable time of fieldworkers in the public assistance program of the State of Maine was used for interviewing. Edward E. Schwartz, *Cost Analysis and Performance Budgeting in Child Welfare and Public Assistance* (New York: Laurin Hyde Associates, May 1962), Table 18.

field interviews made, but also field visits attempted but not made because the client or other interviewee could not be located. For this and other reasons the activity count is an indicator of staff efforts to provide service and not necessarily of service actually provided. Some of the most important dimensions of the staff interviewing effort are presented in the tables that follow.

Table 10

Interviews Reported September 1, 1963—March 31, 1965, by Type and Aim (percentage)

Type of Interview	Total	Aim of Interview: Financial services	Aim of Interview: Welfare services
Total number	*46,769*	*21,000*	*25,769*
Field interviews	*62.3*	*75.5*	*51.5*
Completed	51.0	60.0	43.6
Attempted	11.3	15.5	7.9
Office interviews	*13.0*	*10.3*	*15.2*
With appointment	6.2	5.2	7.0
Without appointment	6.8	5.1	8.2
Telephone interviews	*24.7*	*14.2*	*33.3*
Worker-initiated	7.7	4.1	10.7
Other	17.0	10.1	22.6

AIM AND TYPE OF INTERVIEW | Table 10 shows the distribution of interviews reported by aim and type of interview. The aim is the intended focus or major purpose of the worker when he went into the interview.

Two major classes of aims were identified, financial service and welfare services. A third major class—other official requirements—was intended for the reporting of interviews made by the field staff to fulfill agency investigatory requirements other than those relating to initial determination of eligibility, amount of grant, or the periodic redetermination of these matters. The researchers' expectation based on the experience in the tooling-up period was that interviews that would be reported in this classification would be made in connection with "crash" case reviews or other activity of an emergency and temporary nature resulting from legislative or administrative problems such as failure of appropriations or changes in laws, rules, or regulations. As it turned out, however, while a considerable proportion of "desk time" was spent on record review and form preparation for this purpose, the great majority of interviews reported in this category had to do with obtaining information from clients to establish their eligibility for special services. Most of these evaluations were for services desired by clients, such as nursery school service, or seen by staff as being socially desirable, such as placement of children. Interviews and service units reported in this class have therefore been included with those reported as "other welfare services."

Most interviews for financial service are for statutory redetermination of eligibility. State statutes require that public assistance recipients be seen at stated intervals to insure their continued entitlement to the grants they are receiving.

In district offices other than Midway, as in many public assistance offices throughout the country, initial determination of eligibility is made by field staff. However, the research design for the Midway Project called for these to be made by the research staff. Initial determinations were made by the field staff only in a relatively small number of cases. These occurred chiefly in relation to changes in the category of a case already approved —most commonly a change from general assistance to a special type of public assistance. The percentage of total time given to initial determination of eligibility and hence to the major grouping—financial assistance—was therefore, for this reason alone, about 6 percent less for the Midway staff than would be required of public assistance staff in other offices.

The provision of financial assistance is, of course, a welfare service—and a most important one. However, the term welfare service is used in this report (as in many public assistance departments) to mean service to clients other than direct financial assistance. Interviews aimed at welfare services consisted of counseling, providing information, and making arrangements for the client to use facilities both within the department and in specialized agencies.

Table 10 shows that almost two-thirds (62.3 percent) of all interviews reported were field interviews. This becomes a bare majority (51.0 percent) if only completed interviews are considered.

The rate of failure to make contact was higher when the aim of the interview was statutory redetermination of eligibility than in the case of any other purpose. The large majority of these unsuccessful attempts were for home visits with grantees. Although the lack of telephones in clients' homes made it difficult for staff to make appointments for visits, the concentration of incomplete field interviews in the area of statutory redeterminations suggests that staff efforts to make appointments for this purpose may have been somewhat less than for other types of visits and that clients soon established the relationship between an unannounced visit and unpleasantness and tended to avoid both.

The data in Table 10 also show the tendency of staff to rely on field visits (75.5 percent) to a greater extent than on telephone and office interviews (24.5 percent) when providing financial services. In contrast, when providing welfare services, staff relied about equally on field interviews (51.5 percent) and office and telephone interviews (48.5 percent).

One stereotype depicts a worker who spends a large proportion of his time in making home visits as one who is concerned about giving welfare service in addition to satisfying the legal requirements for financial aid, whereas the worker who spends a large proportion of his time at his desk is viewed as engaged in paperwork chiefly related to financial services. The Midway Project experience suggests that these views are not correct. When the data used for Table 10 were recomputed to show percentage distributions of each type of interview by aim, it became clear that the worker making a home visit is somewhat more likely to be engaged in a financial service than in providing welfare services (54 versus 46 percent). (If the Midway field staff had been responsible for all initial eligibility determinations, this observation could undoubtedly have been made with greater force.) The worker conducting a telephone interview or a face-to-face visit in the office is much more likely to be aiming at a welfare than a financial service (71 versus 29 percent).

AIM WITH RESPECT TO REASON INTERVIEWED | Table 11 shows that a larger proportion of interviews with clients were made for the purpose of financial service (47.5 percent) and especially statutory redetermination (28.7 percent) than for interviews with any other group. A smaller proportion of interviews with grantees were for the purpose of providing welfare services than with any other group. The converse was true of the distribution of aims for interviews with "other persons and community agencies." More than 85 percent of the interviews with this group were directed toward welfare services.

Table 11
Interviews Reported September 1, 1963—March 31, 1965, by Interviewee and Aim (percentage)

Aim of Interview	Total	Interviewee				
		Grantee	Other household members	Friends, neighbors, landlord	Other persons and community agencies	Not specified
Total number	*46,769*	*32,923*	*2,817*	*2,500*	*3,231*	*5,298*
Financial services	*44.9*	*47.5*	*33.8*	*26.6*	*14.7*	*61.6*
Initial eligibility determination	6.6	7.1	9.7	5.4	3.1	4.8
Statutory redetermination	28.0	28.7	13.2	13.5	2.5	54.2
Change in basic grant	4.0	4.4	5.3	3.4	2.7	1.6
Supplementary grant	4.0	4.6	3.3	1.8	5.2	.8
Nonreceipt of check	2.3	2.7	2.3	2.5	1.2	.2
Welfare services	*55.1*	*52.5*	*66.2*	*73.4*	*85.3*	*38.4*
Response to client crisis	4.8	3.9	6.7	12.0	12.5	.9
Other	50.3	48.6	59.5	61.4	72.8	37.5

Table 12

Interviews Reported September 1, 1963—March 31, 1965, by Type of Interview and Assistance Category (percentage)

Type of Interview	Total	Assistance Category			
		Old Age Assistance	Aid to the Disabled (including Aid to the Blind)	AFDC (including AFDC-UP)	General assistance
Total number	*46,769*	*4,082*	*5,820*	*30,503*	*6,364*
Field interviews	*62.3*	*62.4*	*61.8*	*63.1*	*58.4*
Completed	51.0	54.2	49.0	51.7	46.8
Attempted	11.3	8.2	12.8	11.4	11.6
Office interviews	*13.0*	*7.0*	*12.6*	*12.5*	*19.6*
With appointment	6.2	2.3	4.6	6.3	9.5
Without appointment	6.8	4.7	8.0	6.2	10.1
Telephone interviews	*24.7*	*30.6*	*25.6*	*24.4*	*22.0*
Worker-initiated	7.7	11.9	9.3	7.1	6.8
Other	17.0	18.7	16.3	17.3	15.2

In general the closer the relationship of the person being interviewed to the grantee, the more likely he is to be sought out by the field staff for information regarding financial service. Conversely, the staff member seeking a resource person to assist in supplying a welfare service tends to favor those with a more distant relationship to the client. This means that most service was given not by working directly with the client, but rather with others for or on behalf of the client. This observation is, of course, congruent with the fact that the greater number of services were directed to specific material or environmental matters and not to intrapsychic processes.

CATEGORY OF ASSISTANCE | Table 12 illustrates one of the more invariant factors described by the interview data. The distribution of interview types seems remarkably similar for the various special types of public assistance. The widest differences are between the distributions for general assistance and Old Age Assistance, especially in the proportion of office

Table 13

Distribution of Field Staff Interviews and Grantees, by Assistance Category (percentage)

Assistance Category	Grantees	Interviews
Aid to Families with Dependent Children (including AFDC–Unemployed Parents)	45.1	65.2
Aid to the Blind and Permanently Disabled	21.2	12.5
Old Age Assistance	20.0	8.7
General assistance	13.7	13.6
Total	100.0	100.0

visits—19.6 percent for general assistance as compared with 7.0 percent for OAA. This results from the fact that general assistance is frequently provided by the district office staff on the basis of office interviews only as a stopgap until field visits can establish eligibility for a special type of assistance. Telephone interviews, which tend to be positively associated with provision of welfare service, constitute only 22 percent of the general assistance interviews as compared with 30.6 percent for OAA.

The percentage distributions of field staff interviews and of grantees in the different categories of assistance are given in Table 13. The distribution of grantees is based on the average number in the various categories in the nineteen-month period. Comparison of the two percentage distributions clearly indicates that interview efforts were relatively high for AFDC and relatively low for Aid to the Blind and Permanently Disabled and OAA. Only for general assistance were interviews approximately proportionate to the number of grantees in the category.

TESTING THE HYPOTHESES: INTERVIEW COUNTS

Table 14 shows the average number of interviews per field staff position by type of work group. In Plan A the performance of

Table 14

Average Number of Interviews Conducted per Staff Position, Midway Office, September 1, 1963—March 31, 1965

Organization of Work Group	Plan A		Plan B	
	Number of positions	Average number of interviews	Number of positions	Average number of interviews
All field staff				
Conventional work groups	12	890	18	727
Experimental teams	12	800	18	745
Difference		−90		+18
Continuers				
Conventional work groups	4	534	8	726
Experimental teams	5	668	10	757
Difference		+134		+31
Other staff				
Conventional work groups	8	1,068	10	727
Experimental teams	7	895	8	730
Difference		−173		+3

the conventional work groups (as measured by the number of interviews conducted) was higher than that of the experimental teams, but not significantly so; in Plan B the performance of the experimental teams was higher, but also not significantly so. The hypotheses concerning work performance are therefore not supported.

When only continuers are considered, however, the average number of interviews for experimental teams remains slightly higher in Plan B than the conventional work group average, and substantially higher in Plan A, suggesting that with continued exposure to the experimental input the team form of organization is supportive of staff performance. The highest averages were reported not by continuers, but by other staff—that is, early leavers and late arrivers—in Plan A.

Detailed inspection of the data confirmed the researchers' impression that late arrivers were chiefly responsible for the high scores. These recruits were quite young, had a high degree of energy, and in the first months of their employment were motivated to respond to the pressure of work with a flurry of activity. The newcomers in Plan B—the low caseload experiment—were not subjected to the same degree of pressure. They seemed to become socialized more rapidly and in particular to conform to the more deliberate pace of veteran members of their work groups. In an administration that valued a high level of interviewing activity, high turnover rates could be viewed as having some positive effects—and turnover in the Midway office and in the department as a whole was indeed high, by any standards.

A finding shown in Table 14 that, at first, was rather unexpected is that the average number of interviews made by continuers is higher in Plan B than in Plan A for both experimental teams and conventional work groups. As field staff members in Plan A gained experience, the pressures of high caseloads appeared not merely to become less effective in supporting a high level of interviewing activity, but actively to discourage it. Given an irreducible amount of paperwork per case, the higher the caseload, the more time and effort given to these duties and the less given to interviewing.

ACTIVITY PATTERNS

The activity data were examined to determine further whether there were differences in the pattern of interviewing followed by experimental teams and by conventional work groups even though there were no significant differences in the volume of work performed. In view of the important impact of caseload reduction already indicated in the analysis of changes in staff morale, and because of the general interest in the effects of caseload size, comparisons were also made of activity patterns emerging from Plan A and Plan B performance data.

A comparison of the percentage distributions of the aim of interviews conducted by the combined work groups in Plan A with that of the combined work groups in Plan B indicates that caseload reduction produced marked differences in the interview aims (see Table 15). Financial services comprised 55.7 percent of all interviews in the high-caseload situation and only 36.6

percent of those in work groups with reduced caseloads. Conversely, the 63.4 percent of all interviews conducted by Plan B field staff that were aimed at providing welfare services stand in distinct contrast to the 44.3 percent of Plan A interviews with this aim. On the other hand, comparison of the distribution of interview aims for combined conventional work groups with the distribution for combined experimental teams shows extremely small differences. Table 15 thus makes clear that caseload assignment is a more potent factor than work group organization in altering staff interviewing patterns. (Data are not broken down for conventional work groups and experimental teams within Plans A and B in Tables 15, 16, and 17 because there are no significant differences among them.) This conclusion is supported by data on type of interview (Table 16), interviews by

Table 15

Interviews Reported September 1, 1963—March 31, 1965, by Type of Work Group and Aim of Interview (percentage)

Aim of Interview	Total	Type of Work Group			
		Plan A	Plan B	Conventional work groups	Experimental teams
Total number	*46,769*	*20,278*	*26,491*	*23,760*	*23,009*
Financial services	*44.9*	*55.7*	*36.6*	*44.1*	*45.7*
Statutory redetermination	28.0	35.9	22.0	26.3	29.8
Other	16.9	19.8	14.6	17.8	15.9
Welfare services	*55.1*	*44.3*	*63.4*	*55.9*	*54.3*
Response to client crisis	4.8	4.4	5.0	5.2	4.3
Other	50.3	39.9	58.4	50.7	50.0

category of assistance received by client (Table 17), and interviewee (Table 18).

SUMMARY DESCRIPTION OF INTERVIEWS

Data on the classification of interviews by aim, type, and interviewee can be used to obtain a summary description of the nature of this kind of activity. The use of seven interview aims (eligibility determination, statutory redetermination, change in basic grant, supplemental funds, nonreceipt of check, crisis service, and other

Table 16

Interviews Reported September 1, 1963—March 31, 1965, by Type of Work Group and Type of Interview (percentage)

Type of Interview	Total	Type of Work Group: Plan A	Plan B	Conventional work groups	Experimental teams
Total number	*46,769*	*20,278*	*26,491*	*23,760*	*23,009*
Field interviews	*62.3*	*59.5*	*64.3*	*61.8*	*62.7*
Completed	51.0	47.0	53.9	51.2	50.6
Attempted	11.3	12.5	10.4	10.6	12.1
Office interviews	*13.0*	*12.9*	*13.1*	*12.8*	*13.2*
With appointment	6.2	5.3	6.9	6.2	6.1
Without appointment	6.8	7.6	6.2	6.6	7.1
Telephone interviews	*24.7*	*27.6*	*22.6*	*25.4*	*24.1*
Worker-initiated	7.7	7.3	8.0	8.0	7.5
Other	17.0	20.3	14.6	17.4	16.6

Table 17

Interviews Reported September 1, 1963—March 31, 1965, by Type of Work Group and Category of Assistance (percentage)

Category of Assistance	Total	Type of Work Group: Plan A	Plan B	Conventional work groups	Experimental teams
Total number	46,769	20,278	26,491	23,760	23,009
Old Age Assistance	8.7	8.9	8.6	8.2	9.3
Aid to the Blind and Permanently Disabled	12.4	11.3	13.3	12.9	11.9
Aid to Families with Dependent Children (including AFDC–Unemployed Parents)	65.3	67.0	64.0	65.5	65.1
General assistance	13.6	12.8	14.1	13.4	13.7

Table 18

Interviews Reported September 1, 1963—March 31, 1965, by Type of Work Group and Interviewee (percentage)

Interviewee	Total	Type of Work Group: Plan A	Plan B	Conventional work groups	Experimental teams
Total number	46,769	20,278	26,491	23,760	23,009
Grantee	70.4	70.2	70.6	70.3	70.5
Other household members	6.0	5.5	6.4	6.4	5.6
Friend, neighbor, landlord	5.4	5.5	5.2	5.9	4.8
Other persons and community agencies	6.9	6.3	7.4	6.8	7.0
Not specified	11.3	12.5	10.4	10.6	12.1

welfare services), four types of interviews (field, attempted field, office, and telephone), and two classes of interviewees (grantee and other) yields fifty-six combinations. Eight combinations account for 75 percent of the 46,769 interviews reported:

Interview Classification		Percentage
Statutory redetermination	Field, grantee	19.5
	Field, attempted	6.1
Other welfare services	Field, grantee	18.6
	Field, other	4.5
	Field, attempted	4.3
	Telephone, grantee	9.5
	Telephone, other	6.3
	Office, grantee	6.2

RELATION OF UNITS OF ACTIVITY TO UNITS OF SERVICE

The completion of a task by a worker involves not only interviewing but planning, travel, recording, and other activities. In the work measurement procedure used in this research, however, inasmuch as the interview count was selected as the criterion of activity, the work or service unit consists entirely of the one or more interviews conducted in the course of providing a service.

A unit of service provided by field staff begins with an interview made in response to a request from a member of the client system, to meet an agency requirement, or on the initiative of a field staff member. The unit of service includes the opening interview and all subsequent interviews, if any, in the same series that are considered by the worker to be of importance in his effort to provide a service to a given individual or family in relation to a specified central problem. A subsequent interview is considered to be in the same series if it is conducted within four weeks of the preceding interview or after a longer lapse of time if the worker specifically judges that the interview was an integral part of work on a unit of service previously initiated. A unit of service is therefore ended when (1) the staff member decides that no further work is to be done at the time on the central

Table 19

Focus of Service by Number of Activities per Service Unit (percentage)

		Number of Activities per Service Unit					
Focus of Service	Total number	One	Two	Three	Four	Five	Six or more
Financial services	12,718	59.8	22.3	9.3	4.2	1.9	2.5
Initial eligibility determination	1,355	44.8	26.9	11.7	7.8	3.3	5.5
Statutory redetermination	7,643	64.2	21.3	8.3	3.0	1.5	1.7
Change in basic grant	1,486	56.1	22.5	10.6	5.1	2.8	2.9
Supplementary grant	1,610	55.4	22.3	10.7	5.5	2.3	3.8
Nonreceipt of check	624	58.6	23.4	9.3	4.7	1.8	2.2
Welfare Services	11,728	58.4	20.3	9.5	5.0	2.5	4.3
Response to client crisis	925	43.4	21.0	12.0	7.2	4.5	11.9
Other welfare services	10,803	59.5	20.3	9.3	4.8	2.4	3.7
Total (financial and welfare services)	24,446	59.0	21.4	9.4	4.6	2.2	3.4

problem or (2) more than four weeks have elapsed without an interview and without there being a specific plan for one. The staff member initiating the service may decide that the initiating aim is in fact the central problem to which service is directed or that the central problem is different from the initiating aim.

In general a service unit is considered to have ended when there is a shift from work by one worker on one central problem to work on another problem with respect to the same client. The only exception is when a staff member is working on both a statutory redetermination and some other problem. The other problem is to be reported as the central problem, but the worker is not to report the service as ended before he has completed work on both this problem and the statutory redetermination. This rule tends, of course, to understate the volume of work on statutory redeterminations of eligibility and hence on financial service and to overstate work on welfare services. It was decided that this bias was preferable to the opposite one because of the researchers' greater interest in obtaining data on the effect of staff organization on the provision of welfare services.

The 46,769 interviews reported by the Midway field staff during the period September 1, 1963–March 31, 1965, were collated into 24,446 service units for an average of 1.9 interviews per service unit. The average monthly number of cases reported as served during the period was 3,000. This meant an average of .8 interviews per month per client or one interview approximately every five weeks, or an average of .4 services per month per client. The percentage of all service units reported as completed with specified numbers of interviews is shown in Table 19. (It should be kept in mind that the difficulties in fully implementing the work measurement procedures resulted in an understatement of interviews and services provided.)

Over 80 percent of the reported service units were completed with two interviews and 90 percent with three interviews. The activity structure of service units is therefore likely to be quite simple. Nevertheless the fact that as many as 41 percent of all work units required more than one activity argues for the usefulness of a measure such as the service unit that describes the interrelationship of activities in some functional way. The time interval covered by service units—that is, the elapsed time between the dates of the first and last interviews in the service—is shown in the following distribution:

Time Interval	Cumulative Percentage of Service Units Completed
One day	62.3
One week	75.8
Two weeks	85.0
Four weeks	93.1
Eight weeks	98.3
More than eight weeks	100.0

Table 20

Service Units Reported September 1, 1963—March 31, 1965, by Focus of Service and Days Spanned [a]

Focus of Service	Total number	Days Spanned (percentage)			
		1–7	8–14	15–28	29 or more
Financial services	12,718	75.8	9.6	8.0	6.6
Initial eligibility determination	1,355	68.7	11.8	11.2	8.3
Statutory redetermination	7,643	77.3	9.5	7.1	6.1
Change in basic grant	1,486	73.9	9.0	9.4	7.7
Supplementary grant	1,610	74.2	9.5	9.2	7.1
Nonreceipt of check	624	82.5	7.4	5.8	4.3
Welfare services	11,728	75.9	8.4	8.4	7.3
Response to client crisis	925	74.3	9.3	9.2	7.2
Other welfare services	10,803	76.0	8.4	8.3	7.3
Total (financial and welfare services)	24,446	75.8	9.1	8.2	6.9

[a] The focus of the service is the central problem as determined by the field staff member after the service has been given.

The 62.3 percent of all service units completed in one day include not only all one-interview service units, but almost one-fifth of the two-interview service units. Most of the service units that were completed in between four and eight weeks were those that were terminated because four weeks had elapsed without an interview. The data therefore indicate that approximately 98 percent of all service units were provided within a month. Service units are thus both simple in structure and relatively brief in duration. The distribution of the 24,446 service units by focus of service, or central problem worked on, is as follows:

Focus of Service	Percentage Distribution
Financial services	52.0
Initial eligibility determination	5.5[a]
Statutory redetermination	31.3
Change in basic grant	6.1
Supplementary grant	6.6
Nonreceipt of check	2.5
Welfare services	48.0

[a] These eligibility determinations were for a second type of assistance for clients already receiving temporary grants of general assistance.

The average number of interviews was 1.7 for a financial service unit and 2.2 for welfare service.

The distribution of the number of activities varies widely for different service focuses, as shown in Table 19. For example, 64 percent of all statutory redetermination units were completed in one interview, and less than 2 percent required six or more interviews, whereas only 43 percent of crisis services were handled in one interview and almost 12 percent required six or more interviews.

Those services that require the fewest number of interviews are, of course, completed in the shortest time span. Services focusing on statutory redetermination and nonreceipt of check involved the highest proportion of one- and two-interview units. As shown in Table 20, these are the services for which the largest proportion of units are completed within one week. The service focuses requiring the largest number of interviews—response to client crisis, initial eligibility determination, supplementary grants, and change in basic grant—are those requiring the longest time span for completion. The average time span for completing financial services and welfare services was about the same and the difference between these two major types of service was considerably less, for example, than the differences between the two subclasses of financial service—initial eligibility determination and services in connection with clients' nonreceipt of checks.

The distribution of service units by aim was as follows:

Aim of Service	Percentage Distribution
Financial services	54.2
Initial eligibility determination	5.8
Statutory redetermination	34.6
Change in basic grant	2.6
Supplementary grant	5.5
Nonreceipt of check	5.7
Welfare services	45.8
Response to client crisis	3.4
Other welfare services	42.4

In 12.7 percent of the 24,446 service units reported, the field staff member decided after the completion of the service that the central problem worked on was different from the one identified after the first interview. Considering only the 9,023 service units consisting of more than one activity and hence subject to a change from the original to a reconsidered focus, change in focus was reported in more than one-third (34.4 percent) of the cases.[6]

A comparison of the distribution of service units by aim with the distribution by focus of service indicates a net shift of 2 percent from financial services to welfare services. The detail behind the categories of welfare service classified as "crisis" and "other welfare services" indicates something of the nature of the services provided. The kinds of crises to which the field staff responded were as follows:

Crisis Area	Percentage Distribution
Medical	31.3
Housing	29.2
Financial	14.6
Family relationships	9.8
Authoritarian contact (police, courts)	5.9
Employment	3.3
School	2.7
Other	3.2

6. The reporting instruction described earlier (*see* pp. 74–75) produced an artifact in the statistics that accounts for part of this shift.

Medical and housing problems thus accounted for over 60 percent of the crises. Medical crises included those arising from physical and mental illness and from the death of a family member. The most frequent kind of housing crisis was threatened or actual loss of housing through eviction or fire. The inadequacy of public assistance and the thin financial edge on which families and individuals dependent on public assistance payments are balanced are indicated by the fact that 15 percent of the crises responded to were financial in nature. Financial crises arose from accidents and misfortunes that in higher income families do not necessarily assume crisis proportions, such as loss of clothing and furniture through repossession by creditors, fire, theft, or loss, or "mismanagement" of funds. Mismanagement could include paying more for rent than was allowed by departmental regulations, which was not uncommon for large families.

A major distinction between services in response to crisis and other welfare services is that crisis services are almost always initiated by the client or someone within the client system, whereas other welfare services are usually initiated by the field staff member on the basis of his own observations and discussions with the client. The distribution of problems to which "other welfare services" were directed is as follows:

Problem Areas	Percentage Distribution
Medical	35.6
Family relationships	24.8
Housing	21.0
Employment	10.2
School	8.4

Some problems, such as medical and housing problems, are leading problems in both responses to crisis and other welfare services. Others, like financial crises and those involving authoritarian contact, are not of a nature amenable to staff initiative. However, family relationships and, to a lesser extent, employment and school problems are more important parts of "other welfare services" than of "crisis services," and so appear to represent areas of opportunity for staff-initiated preventive, restorative, and supportive services.

TESTING THE HYPOTHESES: WORK UNIT COUNTS

A comparison of service units provided by the different types of work groups is shown in Table 21. As in the comparison of activity units (Table 14), none of the differences for all field staff is significant. The direction of the differences between experimental and conventional work groups for all staff members is the same in the two tables.

The researchers' hypotheses concerning the performance of more work by experimental teams are therefore not supported on the basis of comparisons of either activity (interviews) or work unit counts. Weighting of interview counts by the mean time used for their completion by the different types of work groups did not materially change these results.

SUMMARY

Caseload reduction would appear to be a more effective tactic than introduction of the team form of work group organization for both increasing the total number of interviews conducted and the proportion of all interviews directed at welfare services.

Field staff work was classified into financial services and welfare services to distinguish between staff work directed toward satisfying departmental requirements with regard to restricting the amount of expenditures for assistance payments and staff work directed more positively toward the welfare of clients. This division was, however, only partially successful. A considerable amount of staff time reported as spent on "supplementary grant" and "change in basic grant" represented staff efforts to use agency regulations and resources in favor of clients' interests.

The proportion of the work of the Midway field staff reported as spent on welfare services is higher than would be expected in other district offices because (1) the Midway field staff did not carry the chief responsibility for determining initial eligibility, (2) the caseloads of half the staff were reduced, and (3) there were certain artifacts in the reporting procedures. However, since these and other limitations tended to fall with equal effect on the experimental and conventional work groups, it is believed

Table 21

Average Number of Service Units Completed September 1, 1963—March 31, 1965, by Type of Work Group

Organization of Work Group	Plan A		Plan B	
	Number of positions	Average number of service units	Number of positions	Average number of service units
All field staff				
Conventional work groups	12	480	18	370
Experimental teams	12	430	18	381
Difference		—50		+11
Continuers				
Conventional work groups	4	373	8	374
Experimental teams	5	354	10	381
Difference		—19		+7
Other staff				
Conventional work groups	8	534	10	366
Experimental teams	7	485	8	382
Difference		—49		+16

that the work measurement procedure satisfied its chief function of comparing both the volume and some of the characteristics of work performed by the different types of work groups.

The conversion of interview counts into service counts did not contribute additional information to the comparison of the volume of work performed by the different types of work groups in the Midway office. However, it did demonstrate some of the potential of the work measurement system in providing a description of the work of a public assistance field staff within a problem-solving framework.

The data presented thus far do not support the hypotheses (1) that the experimental team form of organization will provide a work situation that would engender higher morale in its members than would the conventional work group or (2) that the experimental teams would produce more work. The remaining hypothesis to be tested is that clients served by experimental teams will show more positive change.

Chapter Four

CHANGES IN FAMILIES AND INDIVIDUALS

The third criterion used to assess the outcome of the Midway experiment was improvement of or deterioration in client situations. The researchers hypothesized that clients receiving service from experimental teams would show greater improvement or less deterioration than clients receiving service from conventional work groups. A subhypothesis was that differences in favor of experimental cases would be greater in a low-caseload situation than in a high-caseload situation.

The decision to study client change was made in 1962 with full awareness of the profound difficulties involved in the design and operation of this aspect of the Midway Project. The first and most obvious difficulty was the absence of standardized instruments that would yield standardized scores of change for use in social work research. Another was the lack of useful diagnostic typologies with which to consider change in relation to a given type of client or family. A final major difficulty in undertaking study of this area—and this list is by no means exhaustive—was the scarcity of prior research efforts devoted to the study of client change in public welfare.

MOVEMENT STUDIES

Of the then existing studies of client change in social work, the best known by far were the movement studies undertaken at the

Community Service Society (CSS) in New York and first reported by Hunt and Kogan in 1950.[1] In the initial study, termed by Macdonald a "landmark in casework research," [2] movement was defined as "change in the adaptive efficiency in disabling habits and conditions, in verbalized understanding, and in the environmental circumstances of the client in a case which occurs between opening and closing." [3] Other factors such as the degrees to which treatment goals were achieved and casework was responsible for the movement shown in the case, the skill with which the case was managed, and prevention of deterioration were explicitly excluded from this conception.

Movement was rated by caseworker judges on a seven-point scale ranging from —3 to +4. The scale, when applied by persons trained in its use, yields substantially reliable scores. The Movement Scale has, however, a good many limitations that have been forthrightly stated by its authors. Among these is the fact that the movement score says nothing about a client's condition at the initiation or conclusion of treatment. Another limitation is the scale's focus on individual clients rather than on the family. "A summation of individual change does not produce a satisfactory measure of family change." [4]

These limitations led the research group at CSS to undertake a study of the components of movement.[5] This study established the possibility of obtaining reliable ratings among case readers of overall adjustive levels and of various aspects of adjustment. Macdonald, however, complains that the components "lack a desirable unity of dimension, composed as they are of both cause (e.g., emotional health) and effect (e.g., understanding of reality) in levels of social functioning." [6] An obvious severe limitation of both the Movement Scale and the Components of

---

1. Joseph McVicker Hunt and Leonard Kogan, *Measuring Results in Social Casework* (New York: Family Service Association of America, 1950).

2. Mary E. Macdonald, "Social Work Research: A Perspective," in Norman Polansky, ed., *Social Work Research* (Chicago: University of Chicago Press, 1960), p. 17.

3. Hunt and Kogan, op. cit., p. 17.

4. Ann W. Shyne, "Evaluation of Results in Social Work," *Social Work,* Vol. 8, No. 4 (October 1963), p. 26.

5. Ann W. Shyne and Leonard S. Kogan, "A Study of the Components of Movement," *Social Casework,* Vol. 39, No. 6 (June 1958), pp. 333–342.

Movement for research involving public assistance services is the built-in assumption that casework services will be provided by professionally trained caseworkers.

Only one public welfare study has reported the use of the Movement Scale. This study took place in the Marin County (Calif.) Department of Public Welfare, one of the few public assistance departments in the country that is totally staffed by professionally qualified social workers.[7]

THE ST. PAUL STUDIES

Although the studies conducted by the Family-Centered Project of St. Paul were directly concerned with the multiproblem family rather than with public assistance clients per se, many of the clients studied were public welfare recipients. To study client outcomes, the St. Paul research staff devised a "Profile of Family Functioning," using the theoretical framework of social role performance. Social role performance for family members was rated on a seven-point scale in nine areas: family relationships and family unity, child care, health practices, household practices, economic practices, use of community resources, social activities, individual behavior and adjustment, and relationship to the family-centered project worker.[8]

These nine areas, which were regarded as major areas of social functioning, proved to be somewhat interrelated and produced near-scalability scale scores when tested by the Guttman technique—i.e., cases rated favorably in a given area all have higher total scores than those rated unfavorably. With reference to the one aspect, of the studies cited, only the St. Paul study represents an interesting and fairly sophisticated attempt to study

6. Mary E. Macdonald, "Compatibility of Theory and Method: An Analysis of Six Studies," in Ann W. Shyne, ed., *Use of Judgments as Data in Social Work Research* (New York: National Association of Social Workers, 1959), p. 24.

7. "A Study of Marin County, California: Building Services into a Public Assistance Program Can Pay Off" (Sacramento: California State Department of Social Welfare, undated).

8. Ludwig L. Geismar and Beverly Ayres, *Measuring Family Functioning* (St. Paul: Family-Centered Project, 1960), p. 13.

client outcomes. Social role, however, for which some fifty-six different definitions have been advanced, remains a most elusive concept, and Shyne's evaluation of the St. Paul instrument is that "it does not provide a standardized instrument for assessing with any precision improvement in family functioning." [9]

None of the studies summarized thus far used measurement criteria selected specifically for measuring change in public assistance clients. Wiltse, in his study of the effects of intensive casework services on families in which the father was disabled that were receiving Aid to Families with Dependent Children, used as the criterion measure for success (1) employment of the father, (2) active effort by the father to find employment, or (3) the father's involvement in a vocational retraining program.[10] Some public welfare administrators, among others, have suggested that employment and subsequent removal from the assistance rolls constitutes the only valid criterion of successful outcome in public assistance settings.[11] Chaskel suggested that perhaps the most that can be hoped for with respect to change in public assistance clients is a "diminution of crises with crises occurring at less frequent intervals, and with less intensity." [12]

MICHIGAN FIELD EXPERIMENTS

The Thomas-McLeod field experiments in Michigan involving the experimental variation of caseload sizes and the effects of introducing a structured in-service training program used two different approaches to measuring client outcomes. In the initial study the only data presented consisted of changes reported by the caseworkers and recorded on a client information schedule.[13] In the second study, in which more emphasis was placed on con-

9. "Evaluation of Results in Social Work," p. 28.

10. Kermit T. Wiltse, "Social Casework Services in the Aid to Dependent Children Program," *Social Service Review,* Vol. 28, No. 2 (June 1954), pp. 173–185.

11. Raymond Hilliard, director of the Cook County Department of Public Aid, offered this view in an early conference on the Midway Project, December 21, 1961.

12. Ruth Chaskel, "Public Social Policy and Casework Services in Public Welfare," *Social Work,* Vol. 4, No. 4 (October 1959), p. 28.

cepts of reliability and validity of the data, judgments made by an independent observer who saw clients before and after a brief treatment period were used. No scaling or scoring system was attempted, and the results were reported only in the form of such phrases as "forty-two changes in the problem areas of self-support were identified in this group." [14]

Cohen and Bernard, in still another field study in Michigan, studied client outcome as a criterion measure in a study principally concerned with offering intensive casework services to general assistance recipients and an in-service training program to general assistance caseworkers. Judgments of clients' situations as showing improvement, unchanged, or "worse" were made in three global areas: financial status, family relationships and personal adjustment, and use of community resources. These judgments were made by the project supervisor and caseworker assigned to the case. Data were simply reported in statements such as "seven showed improvement in all three areas" or "twelve showed improvement in two areas." [15]

In 1963 Hetzler described an instrument to measure client change in public welfare settings.[16] It involved the scoring of a large number of facts (e.g., presence or absence of electricity in

---

13. Edwin J. Thomas and Donna L. McLeod, *In-Service Training and Reduced Workloads—Experiments in a State Department of Welfare* (New York: Russell Sage Foundation, 1960), pp. 85–88.

14. Donna McLeod and Lydia F. Hylton, *An Evaluation of a Method for Administering In-Service Training in Aid to Dependent Children* (Ann Arbor: University of Michigan School of Social Work, 1958), p. 56.

15. Wilbur J. Cohen and Sydney E. Bernard, *The Prevention and Reduction of Dependency* (Ann Arbor: Washtenaw County Department of Social Welfare, 1961), pp. 92–93.

16. Stanley A. Hetzler, "A Scale for Measuring Case Severity and Case Movement in Public Assistance," *Social Casework,* Vol. 44, No. 5 (May 1963), pp. 445–451.

17. George Lundberg, *Social Research* (New York: Longman's Green & Co., 1946), p. 298.

18. A number of other and, chiefly, more recent efforts at measuring outcomes of efforts to improve family functioning are discussed by Ludwig L. Geismar in "The Rutgers Family Life Improvement Project and Other Outcome Studies," unpublished paper presented at the National Conference on Social Welfare, Chicago, 1970. Among the reports cited by Geismar are the following: John H. Behling, "An Experimental Study to Measure the Effectiveness of Casework Services," unpublished Ph.D. dissertation, Ohio State University, 1961; Geismar and Jane Krisberg, *The Forgotten Neighborhood: Site of an Early Skirmish*

the household) and judgments (such as "adjustment"). The scoring was Lundberg's "sigma" method, which systematically weights the extremes of a frequency distribution.[17] Data were classified by topics, each scored by adding up all the values of the subitems. An overall score was derived in similar fashion by combining the scores of all the topical areas. The topical area scores obviously are weighted by the number of items in the area. If this were seen as a shortcoming in the design of the instrument, its author neglected to so state.

The researchers' modest review of the experience up to the time of the design of the Midway Project experiment indicated that a standardized instrument for measuring the effects of social treatment of clients was not available.[18] An obvious and important difficulty in the movement studies and the St. Paul studies were the attempts to produce an instrument that would have general applicability and utility to the entire field.

THEORETICAL BASE

The position taken in the present research is that criterion measures of the effects of treatment inputs on recipients should be adapted to the type of treatment provided, the treatment settings,

---

in the War on Poverty (Metuchen, N.J.: Scarecrow Press, 1967); *The Area Development Project,* Monographs I, II, and III, and *The Red Door: A Report on Neighborhood Services* (Vancouver, B.C.: United Community Services of the Greater Vancouver Area 1968–69.); P. H. Kuhl, *The Family Center Project and Action Research on Socially Deprived Families* (Copenhagen, Denmark: The Danish National Institute of Social Research, 1969); Geismar, "The Family Life Improvement Project" (New Brunswick, N.J.: Rutgers—The State University, 1970); *New York City Department of Social Service Collaborative Demonstration Project* (New York: Community Service Society, report in preparation). Additional reports evaluating social treatment services that were published subsequent to the design of the Midway Project include the following: Margaret Blenkner et al., *Serving the Aging: An Experiment in Social Work and Public Health Nursing* (New York: Community Service Society, 1964); Henry J. Meyer, Edgar F. Borgatta, and Wyatt C. Jones, *Girls at Vocational High* (New York: Russell Sage Foundation, 1965); A. R. McCabe, *The Pursuit of Promise: A Study of the Intellectually Superior Child in a Socially Deprived Area* (New York: Community Service Society, 1967); William J. Reid and Ann W. Shyne, *Brief and Extended Casework* (New York: Columbia University Press, 1969); Rosa C. Marin, "A Comprehensive Program for Multi-Problem Families," *Report on a Four-Year Controlled Experiment* (Rio Piedras, Puerto Rico: Institute of Carribean Studies, University of Puerto Rico, 1969).

and the population treated. Available evidence indicates that a large proportion of public assistance clients suffer from profound social and psychological impoverishment and disability.[19] It seems unrealistic to expect that these problems can be totally or even substantially eliminated by any one form of intervention and especially by a limited form of direct individual or family social treatment. It might be reasonable to expect that a client's means of coping with or handling a problem, as shown by his actions, will undergo important changes or, perhaps, be activated for the first time. As Geismar and Ayres write:

> We might say that the basic problems faced by the families at referral remained basic problems, actual or potential, though of a lesser intensity. We might say that casework help resulted not so much in marked change in problems as in the family's ability to deal with problems.[20]

An instrument constructed to measure changes in client behavior and situations should, the researchers believe, focus on purposive problem-solving efforts or actions within specific delimited areas of functioning.

The change conception utilized in the Midway study is therefore based on purposive problem-solving actions, as described in Perlman's formulations.[21] Positive change or improvement within this frame is initiation of or increase in purposive problem-solving efforts or change from random, unfocused efforts to more organized activities.

This conception, which was also used by Wiltse, takes into account efforts to achieve change as well as final outcome—that is, in making judgments about change, it allows the caseworker or independent judge to consider client efforts that have not yet

---

19. M. Elaine Burgess and Daniel O. Price, *An American Dependency Challenge* (Chicago: American Public Welfare Association, 1963), pp. 155–201.

20. Ludwig L. Geismar and Beverly Ayres, *Patterns of Change in Problem Families* (St. Paul: Family-Centered Project, 1959), p. 6.

21. Helen Harris Perlman, *Casework: A Problem-Solving Process* (Chicago: University of Chicago Press, 1957). Perlman's formulations also provided much of the base for Ripple's study. Ripple's definition of capacity, for example, "encompasses the abilities which the client may draw on currently, or in the near future, and includes the two main dimensions relevant to the casework process—use of relationship and activity directed toward problem-solving." *See* Lilian Ripple, *Motivation, Capacity and Opportunity* (Chicago: School of Social Service Administration, University of Chicago, 1965), p. 3.

had visible positive outcomes but that give evidence of purposive problem-solving work on the part of the client as well as long-range changes. In Wiltse's study, for example, although the long-range objective might be employment, to consider this as the only outcome of interest and value would be to understate the positives represented by the client's own decision and efforts to seek employment and to overstate the negatives represented by the economic and other social and environmental barriers that are not the target of treatment.[22]

The program of the Cook County Department of Public Aid included vocational rehabilitation and employment services. These services were centrally administered and were available to clients upon referral from the district office staff. They were equally available to clients served by conventional work groups and experimental teams. Such centralized and specialized services were recognized and allowed for as constants in the research design, but no effort was made to evaluate their effects. Interest in the effects of inputs was limited to the services provided to individuals and families by the supervisors and their workers, including, of course, the effects of direct treatment services on clients' efforts to obtain vocational rehabilitation and employment.

A conception of change that included purposive problem-solving efforts by the client is especially useful for study of the effect of treatment services on the clientele of the Midway office, who must almost universally and continuously cope with a formidable array of social, environmental, and psychological problems. They may still have problems after a period of treatment, but they may also have begun problem-solving efforts or have altered their way of attempting to solve them.

This conception is closely related to the concept of limited treatment goals in social casework.

> When casework goals are conceived as complete resolution of problems including those of personality, caseworkers repeatedly find themselves frustrated and defeated. It is this experience that contributes to their self-doubt, to skepticism about their profession, and to assumptions that other professions—notably psychiatry—do achieve "cures" or permanent basic "adjustment." [23]

---

22. Wiltse, op. cit., p. 180.

Long-range goals for public assistance recipients may include rehabilitation (however this is defined), but more immediate and limited goals can be stated in terms of the client's beginning engagement in problem-solving efforts that may ultimately lead to rehabilitation. The decision to seek to sustain a client at a present level of functioning also may represent a modest, limited treatment goal. In considering the aged or disabled client, for example, the client's problem-solving efforts that lead to sustaining his present level of functioning may be studied.

The strong emphasis on action in this conception of change is especially appropriate for public welfare clients for another reason. Kahn describes what happens psychologically when a person applies for public assistance:

> The ego loses part of its functioning capacity; the person's confusion about the changes in his outer world is accompanied by inner confusion, by shrinkage of his ability to operate. A constriction of the ego span occurs, similar to the reaction that takes place when the organism is physically damaged, and the individual becomes oblivious to all but his physical hurt.[24]

Indications of the reaction that Kahn describes were observed by the research staff in the client's seeming apathy in his early contacts with the agency and in his revelation of strong feelings of hopelessness.

Apathy is the result of a long series of assaults and deprivations; it represents an accommodation that has allowed the client to survive. A superb description of this state comes from Leo Rosten's novel *Captain Newman, M.D.*:

> I am convinced that apathy is a distinct syndrome with a specific etiology. Look at it. Apathy follows a long stretch of deprivation; no danger, mind you . . . deprivation . . . bad food, rotten climate, terrible prolonged loneliness. Apathy is a defense against surrendered utter hopelessness. Above all, it follows that awful feeling of having been utterly abandoned. What do I mean by apathy? I mean the state by which all the instinctual drives diminish . . . because of the range and intensity of the regression . . . across the

23. Perlman, op. cit., p. 199.

24. J. P. Kahn, "Attitudes Toward Recipients of Public Assistance," *Social Casework,* Vol. 36, No. 1 (January 1955), p. 364.

> entire libidinal front all the way back to the most primitive state of ego development.[25]

This is a most apt description of the state of mind of those people in the black ghetto of Woodlawn who constituted the majority of the clients of the Midway office. It logically follows that an immediate treatment goal is to help such clients move from a state of apathy into purposive activity directed at problem-solving.

In constructing a frame for making judgments about client movement, Hunt and Kogan came to the conclusion that both action and verbalization should be included (i.e., "movement is change in adaptive efficiency . . . in verbalized understanding").[26] However, the movement studies were conducted in a family agency with an articulate middle-class group of clients.

Hellenbrand and others have cited the lack of verbal skills of the poor and the lack of value placed on verbalization by the poor, observations that were also made by Hollingshead and Redlich.[27] The present researchers' position on client change, therefore, was that a client's action to solve his problems, regardless of whether accompanied by verbalization or objective change in his problems, was an appropriate and sufficient indicator of the effectiveness of service.

Use of this measure involved an assumption—and confidence in the belief—that most people coming to the Midway office, like most other people, are willing and able to engage in problem-solving behavior. Tyler writes:

> There is a good deal of problem-solving among both children and adults of all social classes. The particular problems, the language in which they are couched, and the assumptions made about the factors which cannot be changed vary from one social class to another, probably because of their different situations, and the different conventions regarding "acceptable" behavior. But there is cause for optimism in the indication of large numbers of people

---

25. New York: Harper & Row, 1962, p. 139.

26. Op. cit., p. 17.

27. Shirley C. Hellenbrand, "Client Value Orientations: Implications for Diagnosis and Treatment," *Social Casework*, Vol. 42, No. 2 (February 1961), p. 163; August B. Hollingshead and Frederick C. Redlich, *Social Class and Mental Illness: A Community Study* (New York: John Wiley & Sons, 1958), pp. 308–334.

> in all social classes who have potentialities for developing skill in problem-solving.[28]

It should be clear that in making a decision on criteria for client change, the researchers were not relying on accepting the overt goals of the department's administration, nor was an effort made to ascertain its covert objectives or functions or to study the attitudes and expectations of other interested parties regarding the proper goals of public assistance.[29] Clients' views about what they desired in the way of service and how they perceived what they were getting was seen as an important area for another research project. The selection of criteria reflects a bias in favor of the use of the researchers' professional judgment about valid and feasible (not necessarily most important and certainly not most comprehensive) service goals.

SELECTION OF AREAS FOR STUDY

A conceptualization of the study of client change having been arrived at, the next step was to select areas for study and to construct items for each of these areas. A great variety of criteria have been used in evaluations for psychotherapy. One author has identified "upwards of a hundred criteria used singly and in combination," and she has by no means covered them all.[30] There was also the question of whether to select areas in which data could be gathered and change measured by finite observable criteria, to collect only judgment data, or to collect both.

First, the areas for study had to be selected. The St. Paul study is of interest here. Geismar and Ayres write as follows:

> Eight of the nine areas in the Profile of Family Functioning have to do with the way basic tasks, assumed to be necessary for the

28. Ralph W. Tyler, "Future Prospects of the Behavioral Sciences," in Ozzie G. Simmons, ed., *The Behavioral Sciences: Problems and Prospects* (Boulder, Colo.: Institute of Behavioral Science, 1964), p. 6.

29. As indicated in Chapter 2 information on staff attitudes about public assistance was obtained subsequent to decisions on research design, but this was for purposes other than the selection of measurement criteria on client change.

30. Elizabeth Herzog, *Some Guide Lines for Evaluative Research* (Washington, D.C.: U.S. Department of Health, Education & Welfare, 1951), p. 19.

> maintenance of family unit and welfare of its members, are performed. They deal with the way the family as a whole performs the functions that it is expected to perform.[31]

The selection of areas in the St. Paul study was thus guided by an overriding principle of task and role performance within the family. Others, such as Hetzler, justify the selection of major areas on the basis of problems and needs. "Family health," for example, is included with this justification:

> A number of studies report an unusually high prevalence of poor mental and physical health among the heads of AFDC families. Similarly, a recent study in Montgomery County Ohio revealed that more than a third of the heads of AFDC families suffered frequent and abnormally severe illnesses, and a third were judged to be suffering from mental disturbances ranging from mild neurosis to advanced psychosis.[32]

Cohen and Bernard, on the other hand, give no rationale for the selection of their three major areas for study.[33]

The following is a comparison of the areas selected by the three studies:

St. Paul	Hetzler	Cohen and Bernard
Family relationships and family unity	Family environment	Financial status
Individual behavior and adjustment	Family sexual stability	Family relationships and personal adjustment
Care and training of children	Home integration	Use of community resources
Health problems and practices	Family health	
Economic practices	Employment	
Household practices	Financial management	
Social activities	School progress	
Use of community resources		
Relationship to the family-centered worker		

31. Geismar and Ayres, *Measuring Family Functioning,* p. 11.
32. Hetzler, op. cit., p. 448.
33. Op. cit.

The areas covered by the St. Paul study are obviously the most elaborate and comprehensive of the three studies; those of Cohen and Bernard, the most global and highly summarized. "Family relationships and personal adjustment" by definition includes "the range of personal emotional problems, job attitudes and motivation, marital conflicts, parent-child conflicts, and other of the numerous and complex personal difficulties found in these families." [34]

All three studies considered only families in the selection of major areas for study. The Midway Project's plan was not only to study families, but also individuals receiving Old Age Assistance, Aid to the Blind and Permanently Disabled, and general assistance. The researchers decided to begin the area selection by considering those used in the St. Paul study and to examine in what ways these might be expanded to cover both individuals and families. This decision was influenced by the evidence in the St. Paul studies that the areas could be interrelated into Guttman-like scales. In considering areas, then, the researchers examined individual and family problems, needs, and the possible interrelationship of areas.

One of the nine major areas in the St. Paul study was "family relationships and family unit." This was divided into two subareas—marital relationship and parent-child relationship—following the long-established problem classification scheme of Family Service Association of America. Survey evidence from the Greenleigh report suggested that these areas were of major concern in work with public assistance families.[35] Division into two subareas allowed for the possibility of rating marital relationship in those instances when the family unit consisted of a married couple with no minor children in the home.

Another St. Paul area of study was "health problems and practices." Again, for the Midway study this item was subdivided into (1) health problems and (2) health practices, thus allowing for ratings of positive and negative change in each.

---

34. Ibid., p. 93.

35. "Facts, Fallacies and Future, A Study of the Aid to Dependent Children Program of Cook County, Illinois" (New York: Arthur Greenleigh & Associates, 1960), pp. 37–39. (Mimeographed.)

This too increased the possibility of considering both individuals and families, and the contingency that changes in health practices might occur without a general change in health problems. Anderson and Feldman cite the existence of many chronic health problems among the aged, especially in lower income groups.[36] Greenleigh found many health problems and unmet health needs among AFDC families in Cook County.[37]

In the health area it was decided to include dental problems and practices separately. This is a departure from the general practice of considering these two areas as part of an overall rating. In the exploratory and pilot-testing phases of this project, the research staff had conducted interviews and home visits with public assistance clients living adjacent to the district later to be served by the Midway office. One of the most obvious and striking problems observed was dental neglect. Among the relatively small number of clients seen at that time, a number of adults had never been to a dentist and responded to the presence of dental pain by pulling their own teeth with pliers.

CLIENT POPULATION

Possible populations for studying client change were persons applying for public assistance, those currently receiving assistance, or both. The decision to select cases at intake was influenced by a number of considerations. In order to achieve greater objectivity in data-collection than might be obtained from observations made by agency staff responsible for providing service, it was decided to have social studies of clients made by specialized research staff members who were employed independently of the administering agency. The kind of data required for criteria measuring client change necessitated direct observations of the home situation. To measure change in client situations attributable to differences in staff organization, it was necessary

36. Odin Anderson with Jacob J. Feldman, *Family Medical Costs and Voluntary Health Insurance: A Nationwide Survey* (New York: McGraw-Hill Book Co., 1956), p. 246.

37. Op. cit.

to obtain baseline information on the client's situation as soon as possible after the client appeared at the agency—that is, at intake. To avoid subjecting clients to two different interviewers in close succession, the study plan provided that the research staff rather than the regular district office staff would take responsibility for initial determination of eligibility at intake. Another reason for selecting cases and making baseline studies in this way was to avoid emphasizing to the agency staff the fact that certain cases were being selected for future follow-up, lest special attention be directed to them. Inasmuch as the intake process was not conducted by the district office field staff, the selection of cases at intake was quite unobtrusive. The major disadvantage of this method was that members of the research staff invested a considerable amount of relatively expensive staff time working with applicants who proved ineligible for public assistance. This, together with the expense of training staff in the detailed tasks of eligibility determination, greatly increased the unit cost of the social studies that the researchers were able to use.

Although there might have been some narrow technical advantage to studying only families, there were clear substantive advantages to including individuals receiving assistance through the categorical programs and general assistance. As previously noted, there have been some studies of client change in families receiving AFDC, but none could be found that reported on change in individuals receiving OAA, ABPD, or general assistance. Furthermore, comparison of outcome data on different types of cases—family or individual—might suggest that a given type of work group organization—experimental or conventional—is more effective with one type of case than with another.

A critical decision in defining the study sample was the question of the time span to allow between the initial and follow-up studies. Selection of a twelve-month period represented a judgment based on balancing several factors. On the one hand, in order to strengthen the impact of the experimental input, it would be desirable to provide as long a period of exposure as possible. On the other hand, the longer the interval, the greater the attrition in the number of sample cases because of deaths, transfers, and case closings. The black families that constituted the bulk of the Midway district caseload were subject to community forces that resulted in frequent moves. In many instances cases were transferred to other districts. Moreover, caseload turnover resulting from opening, closing, and reopening cases was high. In preexperimental tests it was found that the intricate and poorly maintained departmental record system made it extremely difficult to trace the case record of a client transferred from one district office to another. It was nearly impossible to locate a client who moved after assistance was terminated.

The Illinois state public assistance plan requires that clients receiving AFDC and families receiving general assistance be seen at least once every three months and that clients in the other categorical programs be seen at least once a year for eligibility redetermination. This means that a year was the minimum period that would assure staff contact with each of the sample cases. The conventional advantages of the year as the period of study include, of course, the dampening of seasonal effects. The decision regarding the period of exposure to the experimental variable meant that an important condition underlying the hypotheses concerning client change was that the families and individuals considered would be those who had received service for at least a year from field staff operating in accordance with a specified type of work organization.

The length of the period during which cases accepted at intake would be included in the study was estimated on the anticipated number of applications that would be received and accepted for service. These estimates, made in 1961, were based on projections of the trend in public assistance caseloads in Cook County. The long-range trend since 1946 had been upward, and the number of cases had increased each year since 1953. However, in the winter of 1961, the trend peaked for both the county and the state. As applications began dropping off in the Midway office, it was found that it would be possible for the research staff not only to remain current with the completion of baseline studies, but also to conduct follow-up studies on those cases accepted after the beginning of the experiment and transferred out of the Midway district or closed before the anniversary of their acceptance for assistance. All cases for which acceptable intake and follow-up studies were made are hereinafter referred to as "study cases"; those study cases that received at least twelve months of service are termed "sample cases."

When the decline in applications persisted, it was decided to extend the period of case inclusion from twelve months to fourteen. Most of the cases that had been transferred out of the Midway district and on which baseline social studies had been completed were family cases. Family cases were defined as those in which one or more children under 18 were in the home at the time of the initial or follow-up study and that received either AFDC, AFDC-UP, or general assistance. Individual cases include all other cases. Classification into family and individual cases seemed to have greater social relevance than classification on the basis of the category of assistance.

In order to protect the size of the sample available for analysis of family situations, especially in Plan B, in the thirteenth and fourteenth months of the experiment social studies were made only for family applicants, and all family cases approved for assistance were assigned to Plan B. This meant that study cases included every case opened in the Midway office during the period February 1, 1963–January 31, 1964, and each family case opened February 1–March 31, 1964, for which a follow-up study was completed following a baseline study at acceptance. The sample cases used for testing hypotheses consisted of all public assistance study cases in the Midway office that were open for at least twelve consecutive months.

The question of the timing of the follow-up study is closely related to the length of the period to which subjects are exposed to the experimental input. Herzog argues that no follow-up study should take place sooner than one year after service ends in order to allow time for "sleeper" effects to become manifest.[38] In view of the potentially high attrition factor in the study population and in view of operating conditions, a protracted delay in follow-up was not feasible. It should be clear that no assumptions or inferences were made concerning persistence of client change.

---

38. Op. cit., p. 55.

TRAINING SOCIAL WORK RESEARCH ANALYSTS

To interview clients and make ratings of their adjustive status and change, eight highly experienced social workers, recruited on a nationwide basis, were added to the research staff as "social work research analysts." Their backgrounds were chiefly in child welfare, family casework, or psychiatric social work. Two of the eight had prior experience in a public welfare agency. No analyst had fewer than five years of casework experience; half had more than twenty. Four of the eight had considerable supervisory experience. All were chosen on the basis of excellence of social work experience, diagnostic ability, and ability to work independently. One analyst joined the research staff in the summer of 1962 to conduct intake interviews and begin preliminary testing of the schedules. The others joined the staff on October 1, 1962. They were given a four-month training period during which they gradually assumed intake staff functions.

Not only were the analysts to make social studies of clients, they were also to complete eligibility studies and to certify clients for assistance. This meant orientation not only to the research, but to the operating agency as well. While the analysts were skilled and experienced diagnosticians, initially they were not familiar with the department's highly detailed rules and procedures with respect to establishment of eligibility and amount of grant. To master these rules and procedures required an enormous investment of time and effort.

The analysts went through the brief orientation in eligibility procedures routinely provided by the department to newly employed fieldworkers. The Midway office intake supervisor and two of the assistant district office administrators provided continuing technical supervision of the analysts' eligibility determination duties and took official responsibility for the financial actions recommended by them.

The analysts were given four months of training by the assistant project director in collection of data on client change. The major components of this training were as follows:

1. Reorientation in interview technique. All analysts came with much experience in casework interviewing but little in re-

Table 22

Extent of Agreement by Judges on Social Studies

Aspect of Social Study	Number of Items	Agreement (percentage)
Overall agreement	60	93.8
Reasons for dependency	11	99.7
Client goals	11	92.7
Physical care	6	95.7
Housing	3	95.7
Housing and financial management	5	96.7
Employment	5	91.4
Mental health and adjustment	3	92.4
Health status	2	92.4
Client relationships	8	88.7
Client vulnerability	6	92.8

search interviewing. The necessity of avoiding "incidental therapeutic input" was given specific attention, and this will be discussed more fully later.[39] Instruction was also given in the purpose and nature of the research data to be used for measuring client change, the interrelationships between the research data and the data required for determination of eligibility, and the possible diagnostic uses of eligibility data.

2. Training in the use of the social study outline and the research instruments. This focused on training in the making of judgments called for by the nature of the scales in the instruments.

Three judges were used to rate the initial and follow-up social studies. First the analyst who had made the study rated it himself. Then two other analysts, randomly selected as check judges, made independent ratings.

The last set of ratings of client change made by the analysts involved bringing together the results of the baseline and follow-up studies to obtain global change scores. By the time the change schedule was used, each analyst had made thousands of

39. The phrase "incidental therapeutic input" was suggested by Wayne Holtzman in a conference with the Midway research staff as a means of identifying any help given clients by the social work analysts as opposed to that given by the agency field staff.

Table 23

Extent of Agreement by Judges on Client Change

Area of Client Functioning	Number of Judgments	Agreement (percentage)
Overall agreement	1,588	88.2
Housing	110	92.7
Physical care	110	78.1
Health problems, adults	110	87.3
children	58	93.1
Health practices, adults	110	87.3
children	58	89.6
Dental problems, adults	110	90.9
children	58	93.1
Dental practices, adults	110	98.1
children	58	100.0
Adjustment, adults	110	81.8
children	58	79.3
Marital relationship	30	73.3
Parent-child relationship	58	82.8
Use of social agencies	110	96.4
Use of recreational agencies	110	100.0
Employment	110	87.3
Household and financial management	110	76.4

judgments on his own cases or on those of other analysts for which he served as check judge. The level of agreement was such that the use of two judges—the analyst who had studied the case and a check analyst—gave sufficient reliability for this segment of the study.

The extent of agreement in ratings of clients' characteristics and situations is shown in Table 22; the extent of agreement in ratings of client change is shown in Table 23. Agreement on the ratings for social studies indicates a high degree of reliability. The level of agreement on the global change scores is not as high as that for the characteristics data because of the more complex nature of the judgments required and because of the weighting system used in arriving at these judgments, but it was deemed sufficiently high for the purposes at hand.

CONTROLLING THE SOCIAL STUDIES

In the problem-solving model for casework practice, treatment is assumed to begin in the first interview. To avoid the possibility of incidental therapeutic input, the analysts were instructed to avoid engaging the client in problem-solving activities. This proved to be a demanding task, especially since many clients had grave crises and others appeared to be profoundly deprived and to have strong feelings of hopelessness and helplessness.

In a few instances it was necessary to take immediate action during the intake procedure to protect a client and/or child from grave danger or death. The following case illustrates this:

> Miss A, recently released from a state mental hospital and the mother of a three-month-old child, applied for AFDC for herself and the child. During the initial interview the analyst noted that the child's skin was quite red in color and had burned patches. When questioned about this, Miss A explained that the child had a cold and that a nurse had suggested steam treatment. To accomplish this treatment, Miss A had suspended the child by his feet over a large pot of boiling water. She was immediately told to stop this.
>
> During the home visit the analyst noted additional burns, and it was quite clear that Miss A was continuing the practice. This situation was reported to the district administrator and the decision was made to remove the child from his mother, who appeared disorganized during the two interviews and whose reality-testing was seen as exceedingly fragmented.
>
> When Miss A refused to admit the analyst to discuss placement of the child and further care for herself, it was necessary to call the police to force an entry. The analyst accompanied Miss A to jail in the police van (relatives were waiting outside the apartment building to take the child), and she was jailed on charges of child neglect. After learning from court officials that a hearing would probably not be held for at least three weeks, the analyst sought out the judge and asked for an immediate hearing. This was granted, and Miss A was moved from the jail to the county hospital neuropsychiatric ward.

All social studies were reviewed, and if the service given by the analyst was deemed to be significant in the treatment of the applicant, as in the case of Miss A, the social study was deemed unacceptable. It was recognized that therapeutic elements may be present in an interview conducted in the most straightforward manner and studies were not discarded because the impact of services appeared to be minor or problematical.

The analysts conducted interviews with 899 applicants for public assistance. Of these 261, or 29 percent, were denied, transferred to other district offices, or otherwise disposed of at intake without acceptance and assignment to field staff; 638 were accepted and assigned to field staff after completion of the initial social study. Of the 638 baseline social studies, 14 were subsequently discarded when a check against agency records indicated that the client had received prior service from the Midway office during the tooling-up period that preceded the experimental period or there was evidence of excessive incidental therapeutic input. Follow-up social studies were completed for 575 cases, or all but 49 of the 624 baseline social studies. The 49 studies were not completed for the following reasons: client could not be located (15 cases), had moved out of the state (15), died (11), refused the interview (5), or was institutionalized (3).

As one means of controlling incidental therapeutic input, the analysts were asked to complete the eligibility certification and to obtain data for the baseline study in no more than two interviews, an office visit and a home visit. This proved impractical in a number of instances. The distribution of office interviews conducted by analysts with study cases for the intake or baseline social study was as follows:

Number of Office Visits	Number of Study Cases ($n=575$)
0	20
1	427
2	103
3	18
4	4
5	3

When no office visit was conducted at intake, it was because of the client's physical inability to come to the district office.

When there was more than one office interview, the usual problem was difficulty in proving eligibility. In these cases the analyst advised the client to return with evidence that would help to clarify the matter. Interviews subsequent to the first were usually not formal diagnostic interviews but brief sessions in which the client presented this additional material.

The distribution of home visits for the 575 initial social studies was as follows:

Number of Home Visits	Number of Cases
1	534
2	40
3	1

Virtually all the second home visits were for one of two reasons: the necessity to see clients who were unable to come to the office or to see the client's children who had not been present in the initial home visit.

The analysts were not told to which work groups their clients had been assigned, and safeguards were established to keep this information from them so that their judgments at the time of follow-up would not be biased. All feasible precautions were taken to isolate the analysts from the agency casework and supervisory staff, and any interaction was strongly discouraged. For example, a separate lunchroom was provided for the analysts. The main concern was to prevent the analysts from learning the names of workers, so that if a client mentioned his worker's name at the time of follow-up, the analyst's subsequent judgment would not be biased by his knowledge of the worker.

Conversely, agency casework and supervisory staff did not know which intake cases would become study cases. At the beginning of the experiment they were told only that the research staff would assume intake functions for an indefinite period and that some of the cases processed would be study cases.

Baseline study information placed in clients' folders by the analysts was limited to the customary, required entries to determine eligibility for financial assistance and the amount to be paid. The workers only learned that a case was a study case at the time of the follow-up visit, when the time selected for the visit was cleared with the caseworker and supervisor.

The analysts reported that in the great majority of cases they were warmly received during the follow-up visit, and clients remembered them clearly from the intake interviews. In all but four cases the follow-up study was made by the same analyst who made the baseline study. One analyst resigned early in the study after completing four initial social studies, and follow-ups on these cases were made by her replacement.

After completion of the baseline social studies, cases were assigned to conventional and experimental work groups in Plans A and B in strict rotational order through a control register. The register was set up to maintain the ratio of 45 cases per worker in Plan B to 90 per worker in Plan A. In the experimental teams cases were, of course, assigned to the supervisor of each group rather than to the individual workers. Shortly after the beginning of the experiment it was decided to assign cases on the basis of total positions, including those vacant, in order to place as few restraints as possible on working out the effects of differences in work group organization—including the effects of staff turnover.

As a result of differential staff turnover in the early months of the project and the effects of the dropping of fourteen cases from the study subsequent to assignment to field staff for reasons previously noted, the number of study cases assigned to and served by experimental groups varied somewhat (but not substantially) from those assigned to and served by conventional work groups in Plans A and B. (See Table 25, page 134.)

STUDY POPULATION, TIME 1

Salient data obtained through the baseline studies are presented in the sections immediately following, including objective material that describes the life situation of people living below the poverty line in a black ghetto and subjective judgments made by social work analysts. The following sections also serve to show how the criteria for judgments concerning client change in the major areas of client functioning were operationalized.

Personal Characteristics

Of the primary clients in the 575 cases studied, 90 percent were black, almost all of whom lived in the Woodlawn area.[40] Most of the white clients—9 percent of the total—were elderly and disabled residents of the Hyde Park–Kenwood area who had not yet been displaced by the urban renewal activities under way in that area. A few white clients still clung to housing in the Woodlawn area that they had occupied for many years and were fearful of losing. The third category represents a small number of Puerto Rican women living in Woodlawn.

The primary clients in 90 percent of the 343 family cases studied were black females, about 6 percent were white females, and the balance were evenly divided between white and black males. Of the 232 cases of individuals, more than 50 percent were black females and 37 percent were black males, with the balance rather evenly between white males and females.

Among family cases, 63 percent of the primary clients were under 30 years of age; among individual cases, 62 percent were 50 or over. The oldest client in the study was 88 years old; the youngest, a 16-year-old unmarried mother. The case of the 88-year-old woman aptly illustrates some of the bureaucratic hurdles that clients must somehow cross in order to receive assistance. The agency intake supervisor had stated that the applicant could not receive assistance until she had given "proof of her age," in spite of the fact that the applicant's appearance provided ample evidence that she was far older than 65. This application was finally approved after the exasperated analyst asked whether a referral could be made to the University of Chicago radioactive carbon laboratory for testing of the client's bones.

The large majority of the families—62 percent—had only one

40. The primary client was defined as the grantee, except in those instances when the grantee was the guardian of a person whose rights had not been restored (as, for example, someone just released from a state mental hospital), in which case the person for whose benefit the grant was intended was considered the primary client. One other exception was in those family cases in which the father was in the home. In these cases the primary client was the mother or mother surrogate. This follows the practice of Burgess and Price in considering the primary client in families receiving public assistance as the mother or the "homemaker." Op. cit., p. 21.

or two children; only 8 percent had more than four. Although slightly more than half of the 311 families with children in the home at the time of the initial study had one or more children born out of wedlock, these families had fewer children than the others, so that two-thirds of all the children in study families were born in wedlock.

The majority of primary clients (61.4 percent) were born in the Deep South states. A considerably larger proportion of family cases (31 percent) than of individual cases (11 percent) had their origins in Illinois. Primary clients in family cases (made up principally of AFDC recipients, the largest and fastest growing of the categories) are younger than those in individual cases. These data suggest that factors associated with dependence on public assistance are now increasingly of the home-grown variety.

In the family case situations, the fact that only 6 percent were classified as divorced, as compared with 39 percent who were separated or deserted, attests to the difficulty poor blacks have in obtaining divorces. While the local branch of the Legal Aid Society offered help in divorce matters, this help was restricted to women who had no illegitimate children and was thus unavailable to many clients.

Primary clients in family situations were both younger and had completed more years of schooling than clients in individual cases. Clients having more than a high school education included a dentist (disbarred from practice), a lawyer with post-law school training, and schoolteachers with postgraduate training. In most instances these clients were seriously disturbed and had chronic, exceedingly debilitating and incapacitating emotional problems. The following case is an example:

> Mr. R, a 47-year-old man who has lived with his 76-year-old mother for the past fifteen years, applied for assistance because his mother had gradually used up the capital from money left by her husband in providing for herself and her son. Mr. R, at one time a brilliant law student who received post-law school fellowships and clerkships with top governmental legal officials, has been diagnosed as chronically schizophrenic. His illness leaves him almost totally unable to function. On a few occasions his behavior has become so bizarre that hospitalization was necessary. His mother has always

signed for his release as soon as possible. Mr. R married during his early career in government, but the marriage ended in divorce because of his mother's interference. His first psychotic break soon followed.

Mr. R spends most of his time playing the piano, but he plays nothing recognizable. He does not speak at all. Prior to the application and during the mother's absence, a telephone repairman came to the apartment and was admitted by Mr. R, but the latter soon attempted to "hold up" the repairman with a toy pistol. The repairman was badly frightened, and the telephone still remains unrepaired.

| Occupations |

Using the standard U.S. Bureau of the Census classification, occupations of primary clients were classified according to the last occupation reported or, in instances when the client reported a number of different occupations, the "predominant" occupation. The service category was expanded to "skilled service" and "other service" to differentiate, for example, cooks and chefs from waitresses and dishwashers and nurse's aides with some formal training from hospital aides without any such training.

The distribution of primary clients' occupations showed a shift from the characteristic blue-collar jobs of the older individual clients in household service and other unskilled labor to the white-collar sales and service jobs of the younger family clients. Included among clients having clerical and sales experience were many women employed by Chicago Loop department stores who were simply released during slack periods and told they would be recalled when there was sufficient work. Assistance payments to these clients obviously constitute an indirect but substantial governmental subsidy to retail establishments. Many of these clients did not seek other types of lower paid, lower status jobs, but remained hopeful that they would be recalled by the stores and seemed to be willing to pay this price for the apparent gains achieved in level of work status and satisfaction.

| Assistance History |

For 64 percent of the family clients and 75 percent of the individual clients, this represented the first application for public assistance. The prior assistance experiences reported by 31 percent of the clients frequently represented several intermittent periods of receiving assistance, suggesting again the casual nature of clients' occupations and possibly the calloused or poorly informed personnel policies of their sometime employers.

The analysts were repeatedly astonished to learn of the strenuous and extended efforts made by clients to avoid applying for public assistance. The end result was that in many instances applications were made at times of serious crisis, such as threatened or actual eviction, when hungry children had not eaten adequate food in weeks, or when the client was completely without shelter of any kind. Public assistance was clearly seen by many clients as a last resort. On the other hand, some clients presented their situations as emergencies in the hope of bypassing the complex eligibility process.

| Housing |

The Woodlawn area, where approximately 90 percent of the study clients lived, is infamous for its ancient, delapidated, overcrowded slum housing units. Any general description of the housing situation in Woodlawn must include the large numbers of apartment houses and apartment hotels. Most of these structures were substantially constructed and in their early history housed an upper-income white population. Now in advanced stages of disrepair and decay, they are part of one of the largest of Chicago's black ghettos.

Both apartment houses and apartment hotels have furnished and unfurnished apartments. The apartment hotels are composed of one- or two-room units, each with a kitchen and bath. The apartment buildings usually consist of units created by converting larger apartments into one- and two-room apartments. In many instances only the rear apartment, originally the kitchen, has full cooking facilities; the others have a small burner or gas stove. The single bathroom per floor is shared by however many families live on that floor.

Rents for housing in black ghettos are notoriously higher than for comparable housing in white slums. Because Woodlawn is in a more attractive location than other ghetto neighborhoods—near Lake Michigan and between two large parks—and because public transportation is easily accessible, rents are higher here than in other sectors of Chicago's Black Belt. Rentals are, in fact, high by almost any standard, averaging $35–$50 per room per month and are exhorbitant considering the state of disrepair of the dwellings and the decay of the neighborhoods in which they are located.

Many buildings have general community reputations—some are known as houses of prostitution; some are called "relief apartments." In the winter months, because so few of the small children have adequate outdoor clothing, the hallways of these buildings swarm with children attempting to play. The unattended elevators in the apartment hotels are a hazard for children, and many deaths have resulted. Peeling lead paint has killed many babies and toddlers. In the summertime, rotting timbers on back porches in upper-story apartments constitute death traps for young children. Usually each tenant has responsibility for taking his own garbage to the basement, although in some buildings there are garbage cans outside each door in the halls where the children play. Hallways are frequently dark, and their walls are bedecked with obscene drawings and other graffiti. The corridors give noisome evidence of the inadequacy of sanitary facilities.

Shortly after the beginning of the field experiment, the Illinois State Legislature placed rental ceilings of $90 a month plus utilities for public assistance families in Cook County. One effect of this ceiling was to force persons receiving or applying for public assistance who were living in high-rent buildings to move when the landlord refused to accept the agency rental ceiling. The search for less-expensive housing usually had to be conducted outside the Midway district.

The largest proportion of the family cases—62 percent—lived in unfurnished apartments. It is notable, however, that 37 percent of the families lived in furnished apartments or rented rooms, again indicating the circumstances to which some families were reduced at the time they applied for assistance. In one of these situations the parents and five children lived in one room, some of them sleeping on the floor. More than one-half (52.5 percent) of the individual cases lived in furnished apartments or rented rooms.

In making an overall judgment about the adequacy of clients' housing, the analysts considered the following questions:

1. *Neighborhood.* Does it lack needed facilities and transportation? Does it pose threats to health or safety? What are other neighborhood qualities?

2. *Building.* Is it dilapidated and unsafe? Is it unsanitary? What are other aspects of the structure?

3. *Housing unit.* Is it overcrowded? Is it inappropriate to the physical condition of the client or any other family member? What are other aspects of the housing unit?

Housing was judged to be adequate in only 28 percent of the family cases and 47 percent of the individual cases.

Judgments were made with respect to housing within the general frame of reference of the presence, absence, increase, or diminution of purposive problem-solving actions taken by the client to improve his housing situation. This framework encompassed not only ultimate outcome (for example, an actual beneficial move), but also situations in which the client had not moved, but had taken a positive action such as applying to the Chicago Housing Authority.

For those clients who changed their residence, the action was considered purposive if the move resulted in an increase in the number of rooms, more control over facilities and space, as in a move from a rented room in another person's home to an apartment, or more homogeneity (fewer or no relatives in the new housing arrangement). The situation was considered to have deteriorated when previously present problem-solving actions diminished or were discontinued or if a move resulted in greater overcrowding or less autonomy. No significant differences in the characteristics of cases assigned to conventional and experimental work groups in Plans A or B were found in the area of housing, physical care, or in any of the remaining areas of family functioning included in the initial social studies.

Physical Care

Physical care as a major topical area is concerned with cleanliness and sanitation, nutrition, adequacy of clothing, and privacy of sleeping arrangements. In making judgments in this area of client functioning, the analysts were trained in the use of standards appropriate to the expectations and available relevant resources and opportunities in the communities in which the clients lived.

The following case illustrates a low level of physical care:

> Miss C and her four young children live in a 2½-room furnished apartment on the first floor of an extremely deteriorated, dirty apartment building. The apartment is in a poor state of repair, with plaster missing from the ceiling and walls. The stove is especially dirty. All four children sleep in one bed in an uncurtained alcove off the living room. Unwashed dishes, empty soda bottles, and dirty rags are scattered at random throughout the apartment. The baby's bottle is passed from mouth to mouth among the three younger children, and during the interview it rolled about on the filthy floor until it was taken up by one of the children and sucked on. The children, who had just had a breakfast of potato chips, were dressed only in dirty, tattered underwear. Miss C is not dissatisfied with either the apartment or the location, and she expresses no wish to move.

Fifteen percent of family cases and 11 percent of individual cases fell in this category. In contrast to the case just described, standards of cleanliness were rated as high in 63 percent of the family cases and 76 percent of the individual cases.

In the area of physical care, the analysts also rated the adequacy of food and nutritional standards and considered the amount and variety of food served and the planfulness involved in food selection. In family cases analysts visited the home during the school lunch hour whenever possible. For almost two-thirds of both family and individual cases, food and nutritional standards were judged to be adequate.

In still another area of physical care, the analysts considered the use made of sleeping rooms on the assumption that a room used only for sleeping is an indication of degree of privacy. Only 43 percent of all cases had such privacy. Less than 40 percent of the family cases met the criterion used by the Chicago Housing Authority in evaluating person–sleeping room ratios: that of two persons to a room.

In making an overall rating of improvement or deterioration, the analysts considered the various areas comprising the major topical area of physical care. Again the judgment frame was the client's purposive problem-solving efforts.

| Health Problems of Adults |

The prevalence of chronic disease, disability, and illness among low-income groups has been well documented by Muller and others.[41] The Greenleigh survey of families in Cook County receiving AFDC found that 64 percent of the grantees had one or more physical problems.[42] Family data in the present study, which describe the situation at the time of application for assistance, show that in 56 percent of all family cases and 90 percent of all individual cases the primary client reported one or more health problems.

The most frequently reported problem in individual cases was hypertension. The most frequently reported health problems of primary clients in individual and family case situations are given below:

Health Problems of Individual Cases (percentage, $n=232$)		Health Problems of Family Cases (percentage, $n=343$)	
Hypertension	29.3	Pregnancy	23.0
Joint diseases	24.1	Disorders of the female genitalia	8.2
Heart disease	22.8	Other	24.5
Endocrine disease	8.6	No health problems	44.3
Eye, ear, mouth disease	7.3		
Allergic disease	6.5		
Other	27.6		
No health problems	9.9		

The rationale for considering pregnancy as a health problem in this population is obvious: The infant mortality rate for the Woodlawn area is 43.7 per 1,000 live births.[43]

While every effort was made by the analysts to verify medical information reported by clients, this was not possible in most cases and the data on health problems must be recognized as

41. Charlotte Muller, "Income and the Receipt of Medical Care," *American Journal of Public Health,* Vol. 40, No. 4 (April 1965), pp. 510–520.

42. Op. cit., p. 60.

43. Spergel and Mundy, op. cit., p. 3.

judgments based largely on subjective reports from clients. In one-fifth of the family cases and one-tenth of the individual cases, clients had sought no help for their medical problems or, having been seen for diagnostic study, they then treated themselves. The following case illustrates this:

> Mrs. W is a grossly obese 47-year-old woman. A year prior to making application for assistance she had been seen for one diagnostic appointment during which it was determined that she suffered from arteriosclerotic heart disease with frequent bouts of congestive heart failure, diabetes mellitus, and chronic cholecystitis. She has had no subsequent medical care, but has kept up the use of insulin because a now-deceased friend left her six bottles of insulin, which she administers herself. She does not diet, and when seen initially had taken a massive dose of epsom salts because she had "galloping miseries around the heart."

The inability of many clients to discuss their health problems and symptoms except in the most fundamental way or with the use of colloquialisms also made the task of making reliable judgments more difficult. On occasion clients showed the analysts areas in which they felt pain.

That more than 90 percent of the clients in individual case situations reported the presence of one or more health problems reflects an outstanding characteristic of this client group. These people were the aged, the disabled, and those too ill to work.

In considering a client's health problems, the analysts rated the degree of incapacity these problems caused. The major criterion used in making this rating was the degree to which the client was able to get around without help and to care for his personal needs. The serious nature of individual clients' health problems is reflected in the fact that 56 percent were rated as highly incapacitated and only 10 percent had no physical incapacities. In family cases, 9 percent of primary clients were highly incapacitated, and an additional 47 percent suffered some incapacity.

Ratings of improvement or deterioration reflected the analysts' judgment about changes in clients' health problems. Whenever possible, judgments were based on verified medical information, but more usually they were based on evaluations of clients' statements about symptoms, pain, and increase or decrease in incapacity.

| Health Problems of Children |

Of the 736 children studied at both Time 1 and Time 2, 81 percent had no symptoms of physical illness at Time 1. Major categories of children's health problems are as follows:

Category (n=141)	Percentage
Infectious disease, respiratory system	22.7
Allergic disease, respiratory system	19.9
Skin disease	13.5
Eye, ear, or mouth disease	11.3
Other illness or disease	32.6

Ratings of children's health problems were made on the same basis as for adults.

| Health Practices of Adults |

Health care for the poor, Glasser writes, consists of a "separate-but-less-equal" medical care system:

> It is a system characterized by charity hospitals, overcrowded outpatient clinics, few coordinated services, shoddy nursing homes, limited availability of private physicians, rare access to specialists, few preventive or early diagnostic and treatment services, and limitations on duration of care more often related to state fiscal considerations than to the needs of patients.[44]

This aptly describes the health care available to Midway clients. The only public medical facility available was Cook County Hospital. This hospital was notorious in the community for the long waiting time for outpatient care and the lack of nursing service in the wards. Other outpatient clinic resources included Provident Hospital and Mercy Hospital (both large, overcrowded, and requiring long waits), Michael Reese Hospital (having variable clinic loads), and the Chicago Osteopathic Hospital.

Two other facilities—Woodlawn Hospital and the University of Chicago Clinics—both geographically accessible to Woodlawn residents, are not primarily community service-oriented facilities. During the course of the study the Lying-In Hospital

44. Melvin A. Glasser, "Extension of Public Welfare Medical Care: Issues of Social Policy," *Social Work,* Vol. 10, No. 4 (October 1965), p. 5.

did, however, contract with the Chicago Board of Health to accept a limited number of AFDC clients for prenatal care, delivery, and postnatal care. Two study clients were included in that program. One other client had health problems of a sufficiently esoteric nature to interest the staff of the University of Chicago Clinics. Clients reported that one clinic—the Tumor Clinic—provided highly individualized attention.

A limited number of physicians in private practice in Woodlawn were available to see clients. These men, known in Woodlawn as "storefront" doctors because their offices were all at street level, were generally refugees or immigrants from Cuba or Mexico. According to the clients, all had a rather limited command of English. All saw a great many patients during the day on a virtual assembly-line basis.

These resources constituted the range of medical facilities available to adult clients. No attempt was made to obtain professionally qualified judgments about the quality of these resources.

At the time of the initial study the analysts rated the usual pattern of medical care in individual and family case situations. For individual case situations, the rating was of the pattern of care of the primary client and spouse (if present). For family case situations, the rating was a composite rating for primary client, spouse (if present), and children. The scale points were as follows:

1. Medical care is generally adequate. Professional help is sought promptly in case of illness, and some attention is given to preventive care.

2. Medical care is provided in the case of illness. Inadequate attention is given to preventive care.

3. Medical care often is not sought until problems reach a state of emergency. Little or no attention is given to preventive care.

The pattern of medical care was considered adequate in over 38 percent of the family cases and 43 percent of the individual cases, or 40 percent of all cases.

In considering change in health practices, the general judgment frame again was engagement of the client in purposive problem-solving actions. For viewing improvement, this meant that the client sought appropriate health resources and followed medical advice. The absence of or diminution in actions to solve health problems was considered to represent deterioration.

| Health Practices of Children |

Nineteen percent of the families had children with health problems; 12 percent of the families had sought medical help for their children. In addition to the range of general health resources available to adults, an additional resource available for young children was the Chicago Board of Health Infant Welfare Station in Woodlawn. This facility provides prenatal and postnatal care, immunizations for infants and young children, and brief-term medical services for young children and infants with minor medical problems.

In considering judgments of improvement or deterioration in the area of health practices, it was possible to consider preventive care, using as evidence of purposive problem-solving actions the client's taking her children for regular immunizations.

| Dental Problems of Adults |

In 49 percent of the family cases and 53 percent of the individual cases, the primary client described one or more symptoms suggestive of dental problems, such as toothache, bleeding gums, loose teeth, and cavities. The actual number of clients with dental problems was undoubtedly much higher, since the symptoms described were fairly gross and some clients with obvious problems denied them. One toothless elderly client boasted that she had no need for dentures and described with some pride her ability to eat whole apples, pecans, and corn on the cob.

Improvement in the area of dental problems was judged to have occurred if the client reported the absence of previously acknowledged dental pain or other symptoms. Deterioration, on the other hand, was rated as having occurred when there was an increase in symptomology or new and additional symptoms were described.

| Dental Practices of Adults |

Dental care for public assistance clients was available at a number of dental school clinics (at Northwestern University, the University of Illinois, and Loyola University), as well as a number of hospital dental clinics (Cook County Hospital and Presbyterian–St. Lukes), and at a clinic operated by a Salvation Army settlement house. None of these was easily accessible to clients and, according to their reports, all appointments tended to be made for the same hour, necessitating long waiting periods. In the dental school clinics work was necessarily slow and time-consuming. A number of private dentists were available in Woodlawn.

The pattern of dental care in all initial social study case situations, like the pattern of medical care, was given a composite rating by the analysts, with the family rating including both client (and spouse, if present) and children. The same "pattern of care" scale was used with scale points defined in similar fashion, as follows:

1. Dental care adequate.
2. Dental care sought only in case of pain.
3. Dental care not sought until dental emergency.

A concentration of ratings in the "dental care not sought until dental emergency" category for both family cases (67 percent) and individual cases (57 percent) reflects fearfulness about dental help, the lack of understanding of the concept of prevention, and a possible tendency to see dental work in a cosmetic rather than a health aspect. Reinforcing these negative attitudes were the paucity of dental resources and the overriding consideration that agency policy did not permit payments for preventive dental care for adults.

Client actions in the area of dental practices formed the basis of rating improvement or deterioration. Seeking dental care for a problem or seeking preventive care indicated improvement. The absence of prior help-seeking actions was viewed as representing deterioration.

Dental Problems and Practices of Children

The presence of a high proportion of quite young children in the study families made this a difficult area for the analysts to explore. Few parents were aware of any dental problems that their children might have, and certainly no gross dental problems were reported. Preventive examinations were supposed to be a part of the Woodlawn school system's health program, but none of the parents in the study seemed to know about them.

Agency regulations permitted preventive dental examinations for children, and in considering ratings of improvement in dental practices, the analysts were able to consider it feasible for parents to seek preventive care for their children.

A composite rating was made for family cases in which the parents and children were both considered. In 10.5 percent of the cases, the pattern of dental care was judged to be "adequate," meaning adequate attention was given both to dental problems and to prevention.

| Adjustment of Adults |

Of all the major topical areas in which measurement of change was attempted, the area of adjustment was the most familiar to the analysts. This was, however, the area presenting the greatest difficulties in terms of the development of judgment criteria. In some evaluative studies the measurement of adjustment appears to be an attempt at what Herzog calls the "ultimate evaluation," meaning (in many instances) a single comprehensive assessment of the effects of treatment or service, or an area-by-area assessment such as considering separately components of personality functioning and then combining the area scores to form an index of adjustment.[45] In other instances an assessment of adjustment may be arrived at by considering a dichotomous presence-absence series of symptoms seen at the beginning of treatment or service and at the time of follow-up. Herzog writes:

> If the purpose requires and justifies a global evaluation, it should be used. But it will have to be used with due recognition of the limitations, and with due respect for the rules of evidence as currently conceived.[46]

Previously used concepts of adjustment seem to be inappropriate for use in a public assistance agency with a paucity of treatment resources and responsibility for assisting clients who in many instances have multiple physical, emotional, and environmental problems. Service given by the public assistance agency is, at best, likely to be aimed at helping clients with pressing physical and environmental problems.

---

45. Op. cit., p. 21.
46. Ibid., pp. 19–20.

For baseline purposes the presence or absence of symptoms of emotional instability in primary clients was rated by the analysts. More than half of the primary clients in both family and individual cases (51 and 52 percent respectively) were judged to present symptoms of emotional instability. Symptoms ranged from frequent periods of depression, fearfulness, and apathy through the whole range of acting-out behaviors to psychophysical disorders such as asthma or migraine. In 5 percent of the 575 cases studied, the primary client was judged to have psychoticlike symptoms or in some instances to be actively hallucinating. Mrs. W is an example:

> Mrs. W is a 53-year-old woman who is applying for assistance because her savings of $600 have been exhausted. Until a year ago she was supported by a common-law spouse, who became ill at that time and returned to his family. During the application interview Mrs. W was upset and frightened, stating that groups of people were "holding meetings on me," had followed her to the office, and were waiting for her to come outside. She says these people have been following her for about two years. She has moved every two months to avoid them, but they always find her. At the time of the home visit, Mrs. W took fifteen minutes to remove all the barricades from her door, saying that even though she had barricaded the door, the "group" might still come down the chimney or through the windows.

Adjustment, as the term was used by the analysts, was by no means viewed as an "ultimate" outcome measure. Positive change or improvement in adjustment was seen simply as the client's initiation of (or increase in) purposive problem-solving actions with consequent increased feelings of self-esteem and confidence. Deterioration was seen in the failure to initiate problem-solving actions, with consequent lapses into apathy, withdrawal, or depression.

The criteria for viewing changes in adjustment, then, were exceedingly modest and obviously closely related to the problem-solving judgment frame in which most of the areas studied were cast. The interrelationships of problem-solving efforts can be seen in considering improvement judged to have taken place in other areas in addition to improvement in adjustment. In 199 of the 204 case situations in which improvement in adjustment was judged to have occurred, improvement was judged to have taken place within at least one other area. The following is an example of an anchor case used in considering improvement in adjustment:

> Mr. J, a 55-year-old man, applied for assistance to supplement his OASDHI check. He was formerly employed as a cook, but both legs had been amputated in 1959. Although he wore prostheses, he was no longer able to work. The prostheses fitted badly, and there was frequent bleeding at the stumps. Much of the time Mr. J could not wear his prostheses at all. In addition he had had no medical care even though he complained of an untreated hernia and dental pain.
>
> Mr. J's room in a converted building was barely large enough for a bed and dresser. He shared the bath with two families. Since he had no cooking facilities, it was necessary for him to eat out. When seen initially he appeared to be quite depressed, lonely, and without motivation toward any rehabilitative effort.
>
> At the follow-up visit Mr. J was in new housing in an apartment hotel, which provided him with a much larger room, private bath, elevator service, a restaurant inside the building, and a hot plate on which he could cook simple meals. His stumps had been treated, better-fitting prostheses had been provided, he had had dental care, and he had made plans to enter the hospital for a hernia repair. He appeared cheerful, spoke of making several friends in the building, and said that he felt "in a better frame of mind."

Adjustment of Children

Assessment of the adjustment of children was made exceedingly difficult by a number of factors. In addition to the large numbers of quite young children in the study families, the precarious situations of many clients when seen initially complicated the study of their children. An important question was the emergence of possible reactive problematic types of behavior on the part of children who might otherwise appear problem free.

Data concerning the parent-child interaction and children's adjustment usually came from one extended home visit. For the purpose of child study it would obviously have been preferable to make a series of home visits, but this was not feasible within the limitations of the project.

Symptoms of difficulty may not be apparent until the child is enrolled in school and finds himself expected to master a complex series of ego tasks, beginning with separation from the mother. Of 736 children studied at the initial and follow-up periods, 391 (53 percent) were not of school age at the time of the initial study.

In addition to the 391 preschool children, 15 others of school age were not attending school. Eight of these children were retarded and had been excluded from school (Woodlawn has few special classrooms for such children), while three others were pregnant teen-age girls. Parents in four families had simply neglected to enroll their children in school.

Of the 330 children in school, 71 percent were judged to have no school problems, 13 percent to have a learning problem only, 4 percent to have a behavioral problem only, and 12 percent to have both. In addition to school problems, the analysts explored other areas in which the child might exhibit symptoms indicative of emotional problems. In 181, or 25 percent, of the 736 children studied, symptoms were found ranging from psychophysical problems to extremely withdrawn states. The most frequently reported symptoms were those suggesting slow development and extreme hostile-aggressive behavior. The percentage of children showing specific symptoms was as follows: [47]

Symptom	Percentage
Slow development	19.9
Hostile-aggressive behavior	19.9
Withdrawn behavior	16.6
Bedwetting	14.9
Predelinquent behavior	13.8
Asthma	11.6
Extreme sibling rivalry	11.0
Skin trouble	10.5
Sleep disturbances	8.8
Speech difficulty	8.3
Other	21.0

47. The sum of the percentages is more than 100 because more than one symptom was reported for some children.

Improvement was judged to have occurred when at the follow-up study there was some indication of diminished intensity of symtomology or when school reports suggested the child was performing better in the classroom.

Assessment of improvement in these children was exceedingly rough and should be viewed as a modest effort to examine small changes in limited areas. The following is an example of a case in which a child's adjustment was judged to have improved, based on evidence of abatement in symptomology:

> Robert is a 10-year-old child born out of wedlock and living with his great grandparents (who are 85 and 88 years of age) and a great aunt, the only employed member of the family. They live in a two-room apartment, and all four sleep in one room—Robert on a sofa bed with his grandmother.
>
> Robert is described as having nightmares, waking up crying and screaming, and as having difficulty in playing with other children. In school, where he is in the third grade, both his grades and behavior are described by the school as unsatisfactory.
>
> At the school's request the grandmother has visited several times. She is still unclear as to what Robert's problems are. In her view he will eventually straighten out; he is just "playful." She sees Robert's learning problem as the result of his having no one to help him with his homework. The grandparents are totally illiterate; the aunt had a sixth-grade education in a southern school.
>
> By the time of the follow-up visit a separate bed had been provided for the boy. The grandmother reported that Robert's sleep disturbances have diminished in intensity and connected this with his having his own bed and thereby getting a "full night's sleep." Robert's grades have improved and his behavioral problems at school have, according to the school, diminished.

Marital Relationship

In 22 percent of the individual cases and 26 percent of the family cases, the spouse was in the home at the time of the initial social study. The analysts reported symptoms of difficulty in the marital relationship in 30 percent of the cases in which the spouse was in the home. The most frequent symptom was open, prolonged, and frequent quarreling.

The analysts additionally rated those cases in which the spouse was in the home at the time of the initial social study but later deserted, or the couple separated. In several instances ratings were made of cases in which the spouse was present at neither study but had again become involved with the family between the two studies. At the time of the second social study there had been a reunion with the previously absent spouse in six cases. In eleven other cases, however, the couples had again separated or the spouse had deserted.

Improvement, then, represented those instances in which the client or spouse had taken purposive actions to resolve problems and conflicts and to restore marital equilibrium. Deterioration was seen as the diminution or continued absence of actions toward improvement of impaired relations or an increase in tensions as reflected in quarreling and overt conflict, brief separations, and desertion.

| Parent-Child Relationship |

The analysts were instructed to make home visits at times when the children could be expected to be at home. Usually the most propitious time for observing mother-child interaction was during the school lunch hour. The generally unsafe conditions of many neighborhoods in the Midway district precluded evening visits or after-school visits during seasons when it got dark early.

An attempt was made to isolate components in the relationship of the mother (or mother surrogate) and the child that could be studied further. Of these the most important was affection. Judgments of the quality of affection given to the children by the mother (or mother surrogate) were distributed as follows: affection freely and naturally given, 54 percent; affection given rarely or not at all, 35 percent; not ratable, 11 percent. Other components studied showing rather similar distributions included parental supervision, expectations, and permissiveness.

Finally, the analysts made an overall rating in an attempt to summarize the general quality of the mother's relationship with her children. The distribution of these judgments was as follows: good, 51 percent; fair, 19 percent; poor, 19 percent; and not rated, 11 percent.

Improvement was judged in terms of the mother's increased

concern for, attention to, and affectionate behavior toward her children or in her more realistic expectations of them. Deterioration was judged as occurring when there was obvious increasing emotional neglect of a child or increasing use of the child to feed the mother's narcissistic and dependency needs leading to her making totally unrealistic and untenable demands on the child.

| Use of Social Agencies |

Social agency resources available to the Woodlawn community were meager. Within the community were a branch of a citywide voluntary family service agency and its legal aid division, the assorted psychiatric facilities of the University of Chicago (although geographically accessible, the admissions and fee policies of these facilities made it extremely difficult for Woodlawn clients to be accepted there), and a division of the citywide planned parenthood agency. The initiation by field staff of client referral to this latter agency was against the rules of the Cook County Department of Public Aid during most of the period of the Midway Project.

Also available, and used with some frequency, was the court service division of the Municipal Court. Clients were referred to this agency for help in obtaining support from absent fathers and husbands. This agency also offered a limited counseling program aimed at helping clients achieve reconciliations with their spouses.

In the year prior to the application for assistance there had been at least one contact with a treatment resource in 5 percent of the family cases. Half of these were with the psychiatric screening facility through which all patients being discharged from state hospitals are supposed to be processed.

The lack of involvement of the client population in community affairs is indicated by the fact that only one of the adults in the sample cases took part in the activities of The Woodlawn Organization (TWO), an active and influential neighborhood community organization. This client took part in a TWO-sponsored rent strike prior to applying for assistance. The lack of involvement by clients in community protest or self-help movements may reflect apathy or fear generated by the widespread belief that protest against the local government or the political machine in power might mean the cutting off of public assistance.

| Use of Recreational Agencies |

Recreational agencies that were fairly accessible to study clients were the Woodlawn Boys Club, the YMCA, and the program of organized recreation at the Jackson Park fieldhouse, including several Golden Age Clubs. Other recreational facilities such as the Hyde Park Neighborhood Youth Clubs, although within the Midway district, were not readily accessible to the bulk of the Midway office clients.

In 5 percent of the 343 family cases, at least one child had made use of the facilities of recreational agencies in the year prior to the application for assistance. Among the individual cases, only one elderly client belonged to the Golden Age groups mentioned, and two clients reported taking part in the organized recreation program conducted in their apartment buildings—a Chicago Housing Authority apartment building for the aged.

While data about the use of the local branch of the public library were not gathered systematically, most analysts made a point to ask about the library and its use. Only one family was found to make use of the library. (For several months during the study period the library window displays along the street of this ghetto area featured books having such titles as *How to Invest Your Money in Stocks and Bonds.*)

| Employment |

The amendments to the public assistance titles of the Social Security Act in the 1950s and 1960s increasingly emphasized and supported services designed to help individuals and families to become self-supporting. Administrators of public aid programs continuously stress the efforts that they like to think their organizations are making in finding employment for clients. The theme of increasing employment is also found in commissioned studies of public aid:

> In almost one-half of the families the possibilities of achieving personal and economic independence within a reasonable period of time were excellent if adequate day-care facilities could be

arranged for the children of some, if vocational training could be provided for others, or if dental or medical care could be provided to correct a condition interfering with employment.[48]

The judgment of "rehabilitation potential" in the Greenleigh study was qualified with a series of contingencies. In the Midway data, on the other hand, baseline ratings were made of the client's motivation for employment and his ability to accept employment. In 41 percent of the cases rated, motivation for employment was judged "moderate" or higher, with little difference between ratings for family and individual cases. However, the present feasibility of employment was judged to be high or moderate in only 32 percent of the family cases and 16 percent of the individual cases.

The results of feasibility judgments took into account client motivation and capacity, attitude toward employment, physical capacity for employment, and the immediate availability of resources for child care. The factors of physical capacity and day care resources were both weighted heavily by the analysts in making judgments of employability of primary clients in family cases, while the factor of physical capacity alone was given heavy weight in considering feasibility of employment for individual clients. A large number of these clients were highly motivated for employment, but were obviously too ill, disabled, or simply too old to make employment a feasible goal.

Judgments about the feasibility of employment related only to the employability of the client, not to the likelihood of his being offered full and steady employment. The analysts' judgments did not take into consideration the availability of jobs open or likely to be open to specific clients. The realism of a client's statement that he was willing and able to work was judged by the analyst in terms of general requirements for holding any job and not with reference to the current status of the labor market for a specific kind of employment. The number and proportion of clients judged to be employable was therefore greatly in excess of those likely to be employed.

Agency policies emphasized the role of the fieldworker in helping a client to become employable or guiding him to employment resources. The Cook County Department of Public Aid had

48. "Facts, Fallacies and Future," p. 23.

developed an extensive employment resource of its own—the Welfare Rehabilitation Service—that offered vocational counseling, testing, job placement, and a variety of training programs. Fieldworkers were required to refer all employable single persons to this service. The Illinois State Employment Service also provided placement services, including screening tests for the longer term Manpower Training Program.

In considering improvement in the area of employment, the problem-solving action frame of reference was again used. Its specific value in the area of employment is that it allows not only consideration of "ultimate" outcome (finding employment), but also consideration of those engaged in purposive action but who are not yet steadily employed, for example, involvement in a training program. Deterioration, in this view, was the diminution of these actions, with a lapse into apathy or hopelessness.

| Household and Financial Management |

Helping clients to improve their household and financial management was considered for decades to be an important area of service. Social work students studying public welfare agency clients were taught the classical technique of helping the client to budget his money by labeling a series of small boxes for specific items of expenditure such as rent, food, and clothing. As used in this report, household and financial management refers to money management, establishing priorities in spending, debts, and patterns of shopping and food buying. The Greenleigh material indicated clearly that AFDC clients wanted and needed help in this area.[49]

It was quite clear that many individuals and families had lived at economic levels substantially below the public assistance level for long periods of time prior to applying for assistance. The Greenleigh data support these impressions:

> Families on ADC, as of May 1960, had supported themselves for an average of more than one year and three months after the occurrence of the major crisis which caused dependency. Financial reserves and credit were exhausted; the mothers worked until they could no longer care for the children and retain a job, or until ill-

49. Ibid., p. 35.

ness forced them to quit. Their relatives may have assisted until they, in turn, could no longer remain solvent and debts piled up. ADC, for the majority, was a last resort—not an immediate answer.[50]

It seems clear, then, that the mere existence of the public assistance check may contribute to improvement in the client's problem-solving actions in the area of household and financial management by allowing him to establish priorities in spending, to shift to more planful shopping and food-buying habits, and by providing relief for at least the most immediately pressing debts, such as back rent. (Agency regulations permitted payment of the previous month's rent.) On the other hand, for those clients accustomed to living above the assistance level, profound difficulties were almost inevitable as they attempted to shift to a lower financial standard.

In 43 percent of all the cases studied the client reported debts ranging from under one hundred dollars to several hundred dollars and, in three instances, several thousand dollars. Fifty-one percent of the family cases and 32 percent of individual cases reported debts.

Another important area of inquiry was patterns of food buying. In 69 percent of all rated cases, the judgment was that the client "carefully planned" his food purchases.

THE COMPREHENSIVE MEASURE OF CLIENT CHANGE

Using the baseline data described, the analysts made global ratings of improvement, no change, and deterioration in each of the eighteen topical areas for family cases and twelve topical areas for individual cases that were applicable to the 575 study cases. Ratings for marital relationship and for topical areas relating to children were applicable in 157 and 307 cases respectively.

Table 24 gives the percentage of cases showing improvement in each topical area, percentage showing deterioration, and the net change—that is, the difference between the two percentages. The topical areas are ranked for each type of case by

50. Ibid.

Table 24

Cases Showing Improvement or Deterioration and Net Change, by Major Topical Area and Type of Case (percentage)[a]

Type of Case and Topical Area	Improvement	Deterioration	Net Change
All cases (n=575)[b]			
Housing	41.4	11.3	30.1
Health practices, adults	34.1	4.2	29.9
Employment	32.7	10.6	22.1
Dental practices, adults	21.0	1.6	19.4
Physical care	26.1	8.7	17.4
Household and financial management	26.8	12.3	14.5
Adjustment, adults	35.5	24.0	11.5
Dental problems, adults	18.6	10.4	8.2
Use of social agencies	6.4	1.2	5.2
Use of recreational agencies	4.0	1.0	3.0
Marital relationship[c]	19.7	20.3	—0.6
Health problems, adults	21.4	29.2	—7.8
Family cases (n=343)			
Housing	47.5	14.6	32.9
Employment	42.8	10.8	32.0
Health practices, children[d]	25.7	2.6	23.1
Health practices, adults	25.6	3.2	22.4
Physical care	25.6	8.4	17.2
Household and financial management	29.4	14.0	15.4
Dental practices, adults	16.9	1.5	15.4
Adjustment, adults	37.3	23.9	13.4
Dental practices, children[d]	14.3	2.6	11.7
Dental problems, adults	15.7	8.4	7.3
Use of social agencies	7.6	2.0	5.6
Use of recreational agencies	6.4	1.2	5.2

the percentage of net change. Thus for family cases the topical areas showing the largest net changes were housing, employment, and health practices; for individual cases, health and dental practices and housing. In general the top-ranking areas were those in which a large percentage of cases showed improvement and relatively few showed deterioration. In a few areas in the middle and lower rank, such as adjustment of adults, marital relationship, and health problems of adults, a respectable proportion of

Table 24 (continued)

Type of Case and Topical Area	Improvement	Deterioration	Net Change
Marital relationship [b]	32.2	27.8	4.4
Dental problems, children [d]	9.8	7.5	2.3
Adjustment, children [d]	21.2	20.5	.7
Parent-child relationship [d]	11.7	16.9	—5.2
Health problems, children [d]	10.7	16.6	—5.9
Health problems, adults	17.2	23.3	—6.1
Individual cases (n=232) [e]			
Health practices	46.5	5.6	40.9
Housing	31.9	6.5	25.4
Dental practices	27.1	1.7	25.4
Physical care	26.7	9.0	17.7
Household and financial management	22.8	9.9	12.9
Dental problems	22.8	13.4	9.4
Adjustment	32.8	24.1	8.7
Employment	17.7	10.3	7.4
Use of social agencies	4.7	0.0	4.7
Use of recreational agencies	.4	.9	—.5
Marital relationship [c]	3.8	13.5	—9.7
Health problems	27.6	37.9	—10.3

[a] For each topical area the difference between 100 percent and the sum of the percentages of cases showing improvement and those showing deterioration equals the percentage of those showing no change.

[b] Topical areas shown under "all cases" are only those shown under both family and individual cases—that is, areas relating only to children are not included.

[c] The number of cases rated for marital relationship was as follows: all cases, 157; family cases, 104; and individual cases, 53.

[d] The number of cases rated for the topical areas relating to children was 307, representing all family cases in which minor children were present at both the beginning and the end of the experiment.

[e] All topical areas for individual cases were in adult cases.

cases showing improvement was balanced or outweighed by those showing deterioration.

Although the largest positive net change in individual cases was in the area of health practices, the largest negative net change was in the area of health problems. The same inverse relationship also appears for adults and for children in family cases. The most likely explanation for these unexpected results is that they represent an artifact of the data-collection process in that the reported improvement in health practices and the reported increase in health problems may both reflect the same increased client concern and awareness of health matters. To the extent that this is the fact and such awareness of health problems is not necessarily an indication of deterioration as assumed in the client change scoring procedures, the index of client change understates the true measure of positive client change. The only other areas in which an inverse relationship might possibly arise because of a suspected common influence of increased client awareness are dental practices and dental problems. However, the data indicate that this did not occur.

All of the eighteen topical areas of family functioning affect children more or less immediately. However, twelve of the topics direct attention to the total family situation or primarily to adults. Five topics refer to children exclusively and a sixth (parent-child relationship) is also oriented toward children. It can be seen from Table 24 that the items relating to children tend to fall in the lower position of family case rankings. The global change score—the average of the net change scores for the six children's categories—was 4.5, compared with 13.8 for adults in family cases and 12.6 for those individual cases. The Table 24 data indicate that the situation of children in public assistance cases is even less favorable than that of adults.

TESTING THE HYPOTHESES

Hypotheses on the effects of the organizational variables on client change, represented by the experimental teams, were examined with the use of global change scores. Global change scores were constructed by using an equal-weight scoring system consisting simply of +1, zero, and —1 for improvement, no change, or deterioration judged to have occurred for each topical area of client functioning. Scores for areas showing improvement and those showing deterioration were algebraically added to obtain a global change score for each case.

Each of the topical areas was scored using the social work analyst's ratings of improvement, no change, and deterioration.

For family cases the range of possible global change scores was from +18, meaning improvement in all eighteen topical areas, to —18, meaning deterioration in all areas. Not all major topical areas were applicable to individual cases, so the range of possible scores for these cases was from +12 to —12.

It should be noted that the extent of the global change score for a given case is limited by the ratings for the case at the time of the initial social study. A change of +18 could occur only in a family for which eighteen topical areas (fields of functioning) had been rated as either zero or minus at the time of the baseline study. Conversely, a change of —18 could occur only in a family for which eighteen topical fields had been rated as zero or plus in the initial study. While the possible range in global change scores was +18 to —18, the actual range turned out to be only —7 to +10, or less than half the possible range.

The global change score is a crude but useful means of arriving at an estimate of overall change in a client or groups of clients. The global change score must be recognized as being a crude measure, because although it is based on an ordinal rather than a cardinal (equal-interval) scale, nevertheless the assumption is made that the change in a family score of +2, for example, is equal to although the opposite of that in a family score of —2. In summarizing scores for a group of cases by topical areas, an area in which almost all cases change to a small extent can show the same net change as one in which large changes occur in a few cases. The global change score is a summation of scores in topical areas, but it must be recognized that these areas are not independent of each other and that a change in one area is frequently related to changes in other areas.

Further, although not all topical areas are of equal importance, because of the lack of any valid basis for evaluating their relative importance, all areas are given equal weight in arriving at the global change scores. However, Lundberg, in defending equal-weight scoring systems, points out that they often give results comparable to those of much more elaborate mathematically derived systems that attempt to factor out weights.[51]

51. Op. cit., p. 291.

Table 25

Study Cases by Number of Months Open Before Follow-up Study, by Type of Case and Work Group Assignment

		Type of Work Group			
		Plan A		Plan B	
Type of Case and Months in Study	Totals	Conventional work group	Experimental team	Conventional work group	Experimental team
Total cases					
Number	575	138	139	143	155
Less than twelve months	261	61	66	70	64
Twelve months	314	77	73	73	91
Mean number of months	9.5	9.4	9.3	9.7	9.7
Family cases					
Number	343	77	72	95	99
Less than twelve months	180	40	42	50	48
Twelve months	163	37	30	45	51
Mean number of months	8.9	9.0	8.5	9.2	9.1
Individual cases					
Number	232	61	67	48	56
Less than twelve months	81	21	24	20	16
Twelve months	151	40	43	28	40
Mean number of months	10.1	9.8	10.2	10.3	10.4

With full recognition of its limitations, the global change score was used to meet the requirements of this research for an index of client change and was computed for all sample cases.

Table 25 shows the division of study cases into those that met the requirement of twelve months of service and so fell into the sample, and those that did not. The proportion of study cases continuing through twelve months of the experiment and thus qualifying for the sample was considerably lower than expected. The high attrition resulted, as has been previously noted, not so much from the closing of cases as from transfer of cases to other districts following the imposition by the state legislature of ceilings on housing rentals. The subsequent difficulty clients had in finding or retaining housing bore much more heavily on family than on individual cases. Of the 343 family cases studied, 163, or less than 48 percent, were in the experiment for twelve months, as compared with 151, or more than 65 percent, of the 232 individual cases studied.

Comparisons of the percentage distributions of the characteristics of all family cases studied (as discussed earlier in this chapter) and of families in the sample revealed no significant differences; the same results were obtained for individual cases. The discussion of the characteristics of study cases therefore also serves to describe clients in the sample when family and individual cases are considered separately.

As with other samples in which selection depends on events occurring in time, the universe that the Midway sample represents is somewhat indeterminate. It is believed to be representative of families and individuals receiving public assistance during the mid-1960s in the Woodlawn area. In ways that the researchers believe are important for social welfare administration, the people in the sample are similar to those receiving public assistance in other northern black ghettos.

| Mean Net Change Scores |

For purposes of testing the hypotheses regarding client change, the comprehensive or global change scores for the 314 sample cases were combined into mean net change scores for cases assigned to conventional work groups and experimental teams in Plans A and B. Mean net change scores were also obtained for family and individual cases, as well as for the total number of cases. The results are shown in Table 26.

For total cases receiving a full year of service, the global mean change score was significantly higher for cases served by experimental teams than for conventional work group cases in both Plans A and B. Hence the central hypothesis concerning client change—namely, that clients receiving service from staff members in experimental teams would show greater improvement or less deterioration than clients receiving service from staff members in conventional work groups—is supported. The second hypothesis—that the superiority of the experimental teams over the conventional work groups would be greater in the Plan B work situation than in Plan A—also proves to be correct,

Table 26

Mean Net Change Scores for Cases Served for Twelve Months, by Family and Individual Cases [a]

Type of Case	Type of Work Group		
	Conventional work group	Experimental team	Difference [b]
Plan A (high caseload)			
Total	0.78	1.77	0.99 [c]
Family	1.68	2.17	0.49
Individual	—0.05	1.44	1.39 [c]
Plan B (low caseload)			
Total	1.62	2.86	1.24 [c]
Family	1.76	2.96	1.20 [c]
Individual	1.46	2.47	1.01

[a] The number of cases is given in Table 25.

[b] Two different tests of significance are used in this table. For testing the differences in Plan B, the Mann-Whitney *U* test was used. This is a rank test that requires at least five ranked groups. Data for six ranked groups are available for Plan B, but for Plan A, only four. Hence the less sensitive rank-sum test was used for Plan A.

[c] $p<0.1$.

but only if differences are considered in absolute rather than in relative or proportional terms.

For Plan A the higher scores for total cases served by experimental teams were primarily due to the significantly more favorable outcomes for individual cases, while in Plan B higher scores for total cases served by the experimental teams were primarily due to the significantly higher scores for family cases. However, even those comparisons that did not show significant differences (family cases in Plan A and individual cases in Plan B) were in the expected direction—that is, scores were higher for clients served by experimental teams. The data shown in Table 26 thus provide clear and consistent evidence of experimental team effectiveness.

Although the primary purpose of the experiment was not to measure the differences in client change resulting from varying the caseload size per worker, Table 26 shows clearly that the mean net change scores in Plan B are uniformly and for total cases substantially higher than in Plan A. However, the following ranking of mean net change scores for total cases by type of work group suggests that the experimental input—the team form of work group organization—had greater positive effect on client change scores than reduced caseload:

Type of Work Group	Mean Net Change Scores
Experimental team, Plan A	2.86
Experimental team, Plan B	1.77
Conventional work group, Plan B	1.62
Conventional work group, Plan A	0.78

| Pattern Analysis |

As a check on the significance of the differences in the global mean net change scores shown in Table 26, a pattern analysis using the sign test was applied to the difference of the net change in each topical area for cases served by conventional work groups and experimental teams. The net change is the difference between the percentage of all cases in each group showing improvement and the percentage showing deterioration in a given topical area. The sign test uses plus and minus signs rather than quantitative measures as its data and thus gives due weight to the cumulative effects of small differences.[52] A summary of results is as follows: For Plan A, total cases, 13 of 18 ($p<.05$); family cases, 9 of 17; individual cases, 10 of 11 ($p<.01$). For Plan B, total cases, 14 of 17 ($p<.01$); family cases, 13 of 17 ($p<.01$); individual cases, 7 of 12. (In this test the number of topical areas reported varies among total, family, and individual cases because ties are omitted.)

The pattern analysis of the distribution of the direction of changes in topical scores thus confirmed the results shown in Table 26 in that (1) the Plan B data provide a powerful demonstration of experimental results for family cases and total cases

52. Sidney Siegal, *Non-parametric Statistics for the Behavioral Sciences* (New York: McGraw-Hill Book Co., 1956), p. 68.

and (2) experimental effectiveness in Plan A is evident for total cases and is especially strong for individual cases.

The topical areas in which significant differences appeared in the mean net change scores of cases receiving twelve months of service from experimental teams as compared with cases served by conventional work groups was explored through the use of a proportions test. Data on percentage of cases showing improve-

Table 27

Topical Areas Showing Significant Favorable Differences for Cases Served by Experimental and Conventional Work Groups in Plans A and B, by Family and Individual Cases

Type of Work Group and Case	Plan A	Plan B
Conventional work groups		
Total cases		Household and financial management [a]
Family cases	Health problems, adults [b]	Household and financial management [b]
Individual cases		Health practices, adults [b]
Experimental teams		
Total cases	Dental practices, adults [a] Dental practices, children [b] Dental problems, adults [a] Health practices, adults [a]	Adjustment, adults [b] Dental practices, adults [b] Dental problems, adults [b]
Family cases	Dental practices, children [b]	Adjustment, adults [b] Dental practices, adults [b] Dental problems, adults [b]
Individual cases	Adjustment, adults [a] Dental practices, adults [b] Dental problems, adults [b] Health practices, adults [a] Health problems, adults [c]	Adjustment, adults [b] Physical care [a]

[a] $p<.1$.
[b] $p<.05$.
[c] $p<.01$.

ment or deterioration in each topical area by work group assignment are summarized in Table 27.

The predominance of favorable results achieved by the experimental team is again made clear for total cases in Plans A and B, for family cases in Plan B, and for individual cases in Plan A. The results of the proportions test (Table 27), which reflect only significant differences in changes in topical fields between clients served by experimental teams and conventional work groups, can now be considered along with the results of the sign test pattern analysis, which indicates the aggregate effects of small change. When these analyses of total cases are considered together, it becomes clear that the general superiority of the experimental team performance results from both a fairly widespread distribution of somewhat favorable change in many topical areas and more substantial change in a few selected areas.

The following summaries of the effects on family and individual cases of the ways in which each of the different types of work groups operated are based on more detailed client change data than appears in Table 27 and on direct observations of the work groups in action. In the high caseload plan (Plan A), client change scores for individual cases served by experimental teams were higher than those for individuals served by conventional work groups in all but two topical areas—use of social agencies and of recreational agencies—and these areas were relatively unimportant in this context because they were found to be applicable to only a few individual cases. The positive effects of classifying cases and making specialized task assignments to workers on the basis of specifically defined presenting problems were apparent in the superior results achieved with individual cases by the experimental teams. Health problems—physical and mental—are obviously central in the life situations of most of the aged and disabled, and the supervisors in Plan A experimental teams tended to assign tasks involving these problems to their most experienced and proficient workers. The effectiveness of this method of case classification and task assignment may be seen in the fact that the largest experimental difference (both absolutely and relatively) shown in Table 26 is for individual cases in Plan A.

Families served by conventional work groups in Plan A did better than those served by experimental teams in the topical areas relating to housing and employment. On the other hand, families served by experimental teams did somewhat better in the area of physical care but even more impressively in the relational and adjustment areas, for example, adjustment of adults, parent-child relations, and adjustment of children. Experimental team supervisors appeared to be in a better position to keep the needs of children in view and to use available staff resources for tasks directed toward meeting some of these needs.

The case classification method used by experimental teams in Plan B did not place as much relative emphasis on health areas as that used in Plan A. The somewhat higher global scores in Plan B for individuals served by experimental teams, as compared with those served by conventional work groups, was the result of significantly higher scores for adjustment of adults and in the topical areas relating to physical care, as well as more modest but still favorable differences in the large majority of other topical areas.

Families served by conventional teams in Plan B did significantly better in household and financial management and considerably better in housing and health practices of children. In addition to achieving significantly higher scores in adjustment of adults and dental problems and practices of adults, families served by experimental teams did somewhat better in eight of the remaining twelve areas. Families served by conventional work groups showed deterioration in parent-child relationships, adjustment of adults, and adjustment of children. Families served by experimental teams managed to show net gains in each of these areas and thus demonstrated the potential of the experimental team form of organization in the low-caseload situation for improvement in areas of personal relationship and adjustment.

| All Study Cases and Combined Cases |

The force of the requirement that to be included in the sample, study cases receive twelve months of service during the experiment can be examined by comparing the sample data on client change given in Table 26 with the data shown in Table 28 for

Table 28

Mean Net Change Scores for All Study Cases, by Type of Work Group, Plans A and B, by Family and Individual Cases [a]

Type of Case	Type of Work Group		
	Conventional	Experimental team	Difference [b]
Plan A (high caseload)			
Total cases	1.36	1.53	0.17
Family cases	1.95	1.68	—0.27
Individual cases	0.61	1.36	0.75 [c]
Plan B (low caseload)			
Total cases	1.42	2.32	0.90 [d]
Family cases	1.46	2.32	0.86 [d]
Individual cases	1.33	2.32	0.99 [d]

[a] The number of cases represented by each mean net change score is given in Table 25.

[b] *See* n. b, Table 26.

[c] $p<0.1$.

[d] $p<0.05$.

all study cases. One effect of the inclusion of all study cases—including those receiving less than twelve months of service during the experiment—in a comparison of global change scores is to weaken the evidence of superior effectiveness of the experimental teams in Plan A; in Plan B the effect is the opposite—that is, it strengthens the evidence of superior experimental effectiveness. The results for Plan A are traceable in part to unexpectedly high scores for cases—especially family cases—receiving less than six months of service from conventional work groups in the high-caseload situation.

When global change scores for Plans A and B are combined, as in Table 29, further light is thrown on the question of the effects of length of service and caseload reduction. For sample cases, the score for total cases served by experimental teams (2.31) is significantly higher than for those served by conventional work groups (1.20). For all study cases, the total score for experimental cases (1.92) is higher—but not significantly

Table 29

Global Mean Net Change Scores for Study Cases Combined for Type of Work Group Providing Service, for Plans A and B, by Type of Case and Length of Service [a]

Type of Case	Scores: Combined plans A and B: Conventional work groups	Experimental teams	Combined experimental and conventional work groups: Plan A	Plan B
All study cases				
Total	1.39	1.92	1.44	1.87 [b]
Family	1.70	2.00	1.81	1.89
Individual	0.97	1.84 [c]	0.98	1.82 [d]
Sample cases (received twelve months of service)				
Total	1.20	2.31 [b]	1.27	2.24
Family	1.72	2.56 [b]	1.92	2.30
Individual	0.79	1.95	0.69	1.96
Other cases (received less than twelve months of service)				
Total	1.63	1.42	1.67	1.45
Family	1.70	1.49	1.76	1.42
Individual	1.52	1.53	1.51	1.54

[a] The number of cases represented by each mean net change score is given in Table 25. *See also* n. b, Table 26.

[b] $p<0.01$.

[c] $p<0.05$.

[d] $p<0.1$.

so—than the 1.39 score for total cases served by conventional work groups.

The effect of the inclusion of short-term cases in comparisons of combined Plan A and Plan B scores is the opposite of that for combined experimental and conventional work group scores. For all study cases, the score of 1.87 for Plan B is significantly higher than the score of 1.44 for Plan A.

Research in a voluntary agency reported by Reid and Shyne subsequent to the completion of the Midway Project indicates that short-term treatment may be the treatment of choice in many situations.[53] As public assistance agencies move toward separation of the administration of financial services from other services, their ability to control the provision of such other services should increase. At the same time the possibility of applying findings of research in short-term welfare services to public assistance cases should also be greater than at present.

The analysis of change scores for all study cases and for combined scores can be summarized as follows:

1. The significantly superior effectiveness of the experimental input in Plan B is confirmed by the analysis of all study cases. This analysis indicated that the experimental input in Plan A was somewhat effective, but not as consistently so as the Plan B input.
2. The superior outcomes obtained by the experimental teams are dependent on twelve months' exposure to service.
3. For all study cases, reduced caseload was a significant factor in raising mean net change scores; the experimental input—the team form of organization—was a favorable factor but not a significant one.
4. For the sample cases, the experimental team form of organization produced significant improvement over the performance of conventional work groups; the reduction of caseloads by 50 percent, which is far more expensive, resulted in some improvement (not significant) over the high-caseload situation.

In general the analysis of all study cases and of combined cases confirms the findings derived from testing the hypotheses concerning client change in the sample cases and extends the possible implications of the experiment.

53. William J. Reid and Ann W. Shyne, *Brief and Extended Casework* (New York: Columbia University Press, 1969).

Chapter Five

CONNECTIONS AND CONCLUSIONS

In this concluding chapter the connections between the bodies of data on staff morale, staff activity, and client change are examined and some of the more salient implications of the findings are specified. Before this is done, however, some remaining questions concerning the design and control of the field experiment are considered as they affect the validity of the experiment and in particular the findings on client outcomes.

Issues concerning the validity of the experimental findings on client outcomes that will be considered here are (1) the choice of the specific areas used in the global scores to measure client change, (2) the training input of the research staff, (3) the addition of unit clerks to the experimental teams, (4) compliance with agency regulations on the provision of financial assistance, and (5) certain supragroup or environmental influences.[1]

SELECTION OF AREAS

The rationale for the selection of areas for studying client change and a discussion of the relationship of the areas selected to those

1. These are the problem areas concerning which cogent questions were raised following publication of the first report on this research. *See* Edward E. Schwartz and William C. Sample, "First Findings from Midway," *Social Service Review*, Vol. 41, No. 2 (June 1967), pp. 113–151.

used in previous studies are presented in Chapter 4, along with a description of how the scores for the different areas were combined into a global score. Would use of measurement criteria developed on a different model and using different components have produced substantially different results?

An answer to this question was sought through a graduate student research project conducted independently of the research staff of the Midway Project. The student project was based on a reanalysis of the previously completed social studies. A subsample of eighty-seven AFDC cases was drawn from the Midway sample of family cases that were receiving AFDC grants and for which social studies had been completed both at the time assistance was initiated and after the family had received assistance for twelve months. After classifying cases into those served by experimental teams and those served by conventional work groups in Plans A and B, the students randomly selected 64 percent of each of the four groups of cases.

The method of reanalysis and a brief summary of the findings given in the project report are as follows:

> An instrument from a different theoretical framework, "The Scale of Adaptive and Adjustive Status" (the "Components of Movement Scale," an elaboration of the "CSS Movement Scale") was adapted and enlarged to measure client change. A high level of reliability (interjudge agreement) was achieved through training sessions. Cases were judged by teams of three students. Teams were changed at random to prevent the formation of response sets, and cases were successfully disguised to hide the nature of the intervention.
>
> Re-analysis of data showed discrepancies from Schwartz and Sample's findings under conditions of high caseload, but agreement under conditions of low caseload. That is, under conditions of high-caseload conventional treatment, a significant number of clients showed improvement in "physical health" and "material circumstances." Under conditions of low caseloads and increased service expectations, clients exposed to conventional modes of service showed improvement only in "over-all" ratings, while clients seen in experimental-team units showed improvement in "occupational efficiency," "physical health," "emotional health," "material circumstances," and "over-all" ratings.
>
> The discrepancy in findings, related to conditions of high case-

> load, may be partially attributed to the difference in theoretical orientation of instruments used in analysis. The "CSS Component of Movement Scale" was intended for use in a family agency oriented primarily toward psychological problems, while Midway is a public assistance agency oriented more toward management problems. With a reduction in caseload, specialized teams seemed better able than conventional work groups to utilize the additional time and move into the psychological and adjustment aspects of clients' lives and were able to effect changes on these dimensions.
>
> Thus, both analyses indicated that a change in organizational form, accompanied by a reduction in caseload, will result in a higher degree of client change than either a simple reduction in caseload size or a change in organization of social work team.[2]

Reanalysis of research data does not, of course, constitute replication, and this modest student research does not constitute a complete validity check, but it does offer some assurance that the findings on client change are not dependent on an eccentric or biased measurement model.

TRAINING OF TEAM MEMBERS

The question to be discussed here is whether the availability of research staff for the training of the experimental team staff constituted a personnel resource that was not available to the conventional work groups and that might constitute a critically important factor in the superior outcomes achieved by clients of the experimental teams. In the early months of the experiment the research staff instructed the experimental team members in the concepts of the team approach and trained the supervisors in case classification and task assignment and consulted with them on evaluating workers and coordinating team resources around the needs and potentials of the families and individuals being served. It had originally been planned to conduct training and consultation of this kind only during the tooling-up period and to terminate it with the beginning of the experiment. However, for various reasons it was found necessary to continue this

2. "Staff Organization in Public Welfare and Client Change: A Reanalysis of the Midway Data," *Social Service Administration Newsletter,* Vol. 14, No. 2 (April 1967), pp. 26–27. Reported by Arthur Schwartz, instructor.

through the early months of the experiment. The training input was tapered off as teams were seen to be operating in accordance with the experimental model. Close observational contact was maintained with both the experimental and conventional work groups, but little special assistance was given to the experimental team members in the last twelve months of the nineteen-month period.

There is no doubt that the training instruction given was not only essential to the conduct of the experiment, but also contributed to the general development of the team supervisors. On the other hand, their performance was handicapped at the beginning for reasons related to the requirements of the experiment. In coming to the Midway office, all the supervisors had professed interest in participating in some kind of research, but they could not then know what would be expected of them. As described in Chapter 1, supervisors were randomly assigned to experimental or conventional work groups. Once assigned, the experimental team supervisors were expected to learn and to conform to methods that were not only different from, but in some cases opposed to, the precepts they had previously been taught concerning good supervisory practice.

When work began with the team supervisors, they made clear that they believed in such classical injunctions as "Don't try to control the treatment of the client by controlling the caseworker. Do invest yourself in the professional development of your workers." Yet the researchers were telling them that to operate as a team supervisor meant not only working through their workers, but also with them. Moreover, they were asked not to attempt to "professionalize" their workers by direct teaching of casework or other social work concepts, but rather to instruct the workers in the specifics of the tasks that they were being asked to perform. The supervisors were to proceed on the premises that (1) the teaching of theory is the function of the universities and (2) each worker would develop as a paraprofessional worker as he and his supervisor agreed that he was ready to undertake an increasingly wider range of tasks of increasingly greater complexity and involving increasing experience, responsibility, creativity, and autonomy. Team supervisors were required to learn and carry out new classification procedures and to plan episodes of service around the needs of clients. Those workers who had become, accustomed, before assignment to experimental teams, to be "in charge of cases" were now required to accept supervision on a task basis.

The researchers believe that although the staff training and consultation provided to the experimental teams was a positive factor, it represented an offset and—all things considered—an inadequate offset for the numerous handicaps imposed on the experimental team members.

THE UNIT CLERK ISSUE

The addition of unit clerks to the experimental teams was part of an effort to carry the idea of differential utilization of personnel as far as was feasible within an autonomous work group structure. In order to emphasize and support the cohesiveness and unity of the group, all members of the team—including the supervisor—were given space in a partitioned office and the team's case records were decentralized to this area. However, the inclusion of the unit clerk in the experimental team raises the question as to what extent this had an effect on the intent to provide equal resources to both types of work groups.

The midpoint of the annual salary ranges at the midpoint of the experimental period were as follows: supervisory caseworker, $6,900; worker, $5,760; unit clerk, $4,500. On this basis, total salaries for an experimental team were 12.6 percent higher than for a conventional work group. However, some of the duties the unit clerks performed for the teams—such as the pulling and filing of case records, making certain kinds of changes in assistance budgets, preparing forms to open records for new cases, and completing arrangements for transferring cases to other districts were performed for the conventional work groups by centralized clerical services. On the other hand, the unit clerks performed some services that were not included in centralized clerical services, such as answering the telephone, obtaining and giving standardized information, and assisting and maintaining desk tickler files for workers.

In order to obtain an estimate of the input of a unit clerk above that of centralized clerical services, a time study was conducted, using a work sampling or "snap observation" procedure.[3] The returns provided the following distribution of unit clerk time:

Allotment of Time	Percentage
Nonsystematic time	40
Absences (vacation, sick leave, other)	12
Personal (not directly related to official duties)	28
Systematic time	60
On duties similar to central clerical services	23
On duties different from central clerical services	37

On the basis of these data, staff input for experimental teams in excess of that for conventional work groups consisting of a supervisor and five workers was the equivalent of little more than one-third of a clerical worker per team. The additional annual cost to the department for this time plus a proportionate share of the cost of nonsystematic time was $2,775. The total salary bill for an experimental team was therefore 7 percent above that for a conventional work group.

The results of the unit clerk time study were discussed with the supervisors in a meeting held after the termination of the experiment. The consensus among the supervisors was that the unit clerk time study data understated the proportion of paid time given to official duties (systematic time) and overstated personal time. The supervisors attributed this to the unit clerks' indifference or resistance to the time study and hence their failure to specify the nature of the work in which they were engaged when queried by the time clerk. (Although the unit clerks were given the same kind of explanation as the field staff at the time their work was analyzed, they may not have understood or trusted the explanation.) If the supervisors' contentions are correct, the estimate of additional clerical resources utilized by the teams is an understatement; the estimate of an additional cost of 7 percent would, however, not be affected. A time study of centralized clerical services was not undertaken; the estimate of additional clerical resources used by the teams is based on the assumption that conventional work groups re-

3. Robert E. Heiland and J. Richardson Wallace, *Work Sampling* (New York: McGraw-Hill Book Co., 1957).

ceived centralized services equal to those of a similar nature received by the teams. This assumption does affect the cost estimate. The researchers believe the assumption is valid because of direct observations that all field staff had as much of this kind of service as they were willing to use.

In order to gain some perspective, and without implying a causal relationship, the 7 percent additional cost may be considered along with the following comparison based on the "payoff criterion": the mean global change score for all sample cases served by conventional work groups was 1.20 and for experimental team cases, 2.31—a difference of more than 92 percent. Neither the work measurement data nor any of the researchers' other observations at Midway provide evidence that relieving team supervisors and workers of some paperwork and routine duties resulted in a significant increase in their interviewing activities or service unit production.

During the tooling-up period and in the early months of the experiment some workers, especially in Plan B, clung to the security of work that they knew how to do and resisted using the unit clerks. An assertion frequently made by these workers was that it took less time to do many of the clerical tasks themselves than to give a unit clerk the necessary instructions. However, before the end of the experiment the function of the unit clerk was well accepted by workers in both Plans A and B.

The researchers' opinion is that the unit clerks made the job somewhat less trying for the experimental team members, and this may have contributed in some way to the superior outcomes they achieved with sample cases, but that the contribution of the unit clerks was in no sense determinative or even important to these outcomes. This opinion relates only to the Midway office experience and not to other efforts to utilize unit clerks in public assistance work groups. The low proportion of total time reported as systematic time for unit clerks (60 percent) may have been due to the lack of adequate training and supervision of the unit clerks in this project.[4] Each clerk was placed under the im-

4. Systematic time reported for all supervisors and workers in the Midway field staff was 81 percent. Hirobumi Uno, "Work Patterns of Work Groups in the Administration of Public Assistance." Unpublished Ph.D. dissertation, University of Chicago School of Social Service Administration, 1966.

mediate direction of the team supervisor rather than under a chief clerk; the researchers continue to believe that this was organizationally sound. However, in retrospect it appears that the provision of more training and continuing technical assistance to the unit clerks and more instruction of the supervisors in how to make the best use of clerical assistance might have resulted in fuller use of the unit clerks.

The tryout of unit clerks in the Midway office helped to stimulate their use elsewhere by the department and an evaluative report of the experience in one of their installations points to quite positive findings.[5]

COMPLIANCE WITH AGENCY REGULATIONS

In the Cook County Department of Public Aid, as in most local public assistance administrations, federal, state, and local rules and regulations concerning procedures for determining applicants' entitlement to assistance payments and the amounts to be paid are passed down to district offices in great detail. Procedures and expectations of referral to certain centralized services such as employment and vocational rehabilitation are also made most specific. The central orientation and training of new staff are almost entirely around the use of the forms involved in providing financial assistance. In contrast to this emphasis on administering financial assistance, a relatively small proportion of departmental resources is invested in instruction of field staff and in the setting of expectations concerning the provision of other services to individuals and families. This function is left largely to the discretion of district office staff.

The researchers' chief concern in this project—in the design of the experiment, the training of field staff for the team form of practice, and the measurement of outcomes—was in the provision of welfare services in addition to financial aid. It is recognized, of course, that the chief investment of time by the field staff was in the provision of financial assistance and that this

5. "The Unit Clerk System: A Recent Evaluation of the Unit Clerk System of Casework Organization at the Stateway Gardens Office," report prepared under the direction of Walter W. Hudson (Chicago: Cook County Department of Public Aid, 1966). (Mimeographed.)

is the base on which other services must be built. Therefore, in an effort to supplement our own observations and criteria on services with those more directly related to outcomes of financial assistance, an arrangement was made through the department for an official audit of the work of the Midway District Office to be conducted by the Illinois Commission on Public Aid under its customary procedures, but with the sampling of cases to be done in a way that might provide some basis for comparing outcomes of the efforts of conventional work groups and experimental teams in both Plans A and B.

The commission conducted a review of a sample of 185 cases representing all cases active on March 1, 1965 (the beginning of the last month of the experiment), except cases receiving only general assistance. The Illinois state review, designed in large part to meet federal requirements, did not include cases receiving only general assistance payments apparently because no federal matching funds were involved in those payments. The review was conducted by the staff of the State Department of Public Aid and included (1) an analysis of information in the case record, (2) an interview with the recipient in his home, and (3) verification of essential data with other informants or sources insofar as this was possible. The results of the review that are relevant for the Midway Project are given in Table 30.

The summary conclusion of the review staff was as follows:

> Review findings for the Midway District Office sample of active categorical cases show grave deficiencies in the implementation of policy and procedures as they relate to the determination of eligibility and the amount of the assistance payments. Service needs have been satisfactorily met in the majority of cases.[6]

After receipt of this report in the Midway office, the research staff received information that challenged the accuracy of many of the findings of the state review. The interest of the research staff in the state review was, however, directed to comparisons of the performance of the different types of work groups in the Midway office and not to the general level of compliance of the

6. "Report of the Division of Special Services, Case Review Section," Illinois Commission on Public Aid, May 1, 1965. (Mimeographed.)

Midway staff with agency regulations on the administration of financial assistance. The type of work group that had provided service to the cases included in the sample given to the state review staff members was identified for them by the research staff only after the state review staff had completed its work, and the researchers are aware of no reason why the results of their review should show any systematic bias in the data comparing the performance of the conventional work groups with that of the experimental teams.

Of the five items used by the state review staff to report its findings, three—ineligible, eligible on basis of case record, and eligible on basis of additional entries by review staff—describe

Table 30

Findings from Illinois Department of Public Aid Review Investigation of a Sample of Cases Active in the Midway District Office in May 1965 [a]

Item	Combined Plans		Plan A		Plan B	
	Conventional work groups	Experimental teams	Conventional work groups	Experimental teams	Conventional work groups	Experimental teams
Ineligible	6	8	5	4	1	4
Eligible on basis of case record	14	7	8	1	6	6
Eligible on basis of additional entries by review staff	—	2	—	1	—	1
Eligibility conditional on findings of future follow-up	36	54	16	32	20	22
Eligibility and/or extent of need inadequately documented	36	22	21	13	15	9
Total number	92	93	50	51	42	42

[a] From Table 1 of the "Report of the Division of Special Services, Case Review Section," Illinois Commission on Public Aid, May 1, 1965. (Mimeographed.)

judgments by the review staff that purport to be conclusive. The last two items in Table 30 represent cases on which final judgments could not be made until more information was obtained.

The judgments on eligibility and ineligibility relate to a function that was not completely or initially the responsibility of the Midway field staff. During the course of the experiment, eligibility of applicants was completed at intake before the assignment of cases to field staff. The remaining and by far the majority of cases under care at the time of the review had been transferred from other district offices after the Midway office was opened. The initial investigation of eligibility on many of these cases had been made two or three years before their transfer to the Midway office. The Midway office field staff, like other departmental field staff, was responsible for periodic verification of eligibility. The focus of staff in the recertification process in the Cook County Department of Public Aid, as in many public assistance agencies, is on any changes that have occurred since the previous investigation or certification. However, as the state review indicates, the agency attempts to hold field staff members responsible for comprehensive reviews of the eligibility of all cases currently assigned to them.

In order to use the state review data on eligibility to make comparisons of work group performance, the researchers adopted the convention of taking the algebraic difference between the number of Midway field staff determinations of eligibility found by the review staff to be correct and the number found to be incorrect, to obtain a count of net correct determinations. This gives the following results:

Type of Work Group	Net Correct Determinations
Combined conventional work groups	+8
Combined experimental teams	+1
Plan A	
Conventional work groups	+3
Experimental teams	−2
Plan B	
Conventional work groups	+5
Experimental teams	+3

The last two items in Table 30 refer to judgments by the state review staff that are quite tentative and indeterminate and the distinction between the two is not without ambiguity. Comparison of the performance of conventional work groups and experimental teams based on each of the items go in diametrically opposed directions, and when the two are combined they tend to cancel each other out. Unequivocal conclusions concerning comparative conformance to state rules and regulations on financial assistance cannot be reached on the basis of the state review data; on the basis of judgments concerning the small number of cases in the first three items in Table 30, it would appear that the quality of the performance of the conventional work groups in determining eligibility was higher than that of the experimental teams.

SUPRAGROUP INFLUENCES

The preceding discussions of the administration of financial assistance, the research staff training inputs, and the unit clerk issue related to the question of whether the superiority in client change scores for cases served by experimental teams can be attributed to the additional resources utilized by the experimental teams. It is possible, on the other hand, to point to some unintended consequences of the experimental situation that appeared to favor the outcomes of cases served by conventional work groups.

For example, Hawthorne effects are usually thought of as exerting an unintended bias in favor of outcomes of experimental or study subjects as opposed to control or comparison subjects. In the course of the Midway Project the researchers became aware of a kind of negative Hawthorne effect that appeared to derive from a competitive reaction on the part of some of the younger workers assigned to conventional work groups. They appeared to be stimulated to report an unusually high level of interviewing activity and service production. One young "rate-buster" stated that he and a select few of his colleagues would show the research staff that "we can do more than your teams." After raising his output more than 2½ times higher than the mean for the field staff as a whole and maintaining this pace for six months, he resigned precipitously with a mixed air of triumph, relief, and disdain.

Despite this kind of sporadic manifestation, the analysis of field staff attitudes as described in Chapter 2 shows that there were no significant differences between experimental and conventional work group members in the way they felt about the research project.

Of far greater importance than factors that appear to have favored either experimental or conventional work groups are those that diluted the effects of intended experimental input, contaminating the conventional work groups with teamlike attributes, or "swamping" the work of the entire field staff, so any differences that might exist in outcomes would be difficult or impossible to measure. Some of these effects and the research staff's efforts to deal with them are described in Chapter 2.[7]

A final example of the researchers' efforts to cope with the threats to the implementation of the research design and the conduct of the experiment is concerned with what might be called the district office superstructure and specifically the levels of control immediately above the supervisor. In the Midway office, as in other district offices, supervisors were immediately responsible to assistant district office supervisors, who were in turn responsible to the district office supervisor. Two assistant district office supervisors were each responsible for four work groups and one supervised two work groups in addition to performing special duties assigned by the district office supervisor.

During the tooling-up period it became evident that the team supervisors were suffering from conflict between their roles as members of the district office staff and as key participants in the field experiment. The research staff was instructing the team supervisors in how they were to arrive at treatment decisions and the assistant district office supervisors were reviewing and sometimes reversing the decisions reached by supervisors of both experimental and conventional work groups. The supervisors assigned to conventional work groups were not affected (or

7. For a fuller development *see* Edward E. Schwartz, "Strategies for Research in Public Welfare Administration: The Field Experiment," *Trends in Social Work Practice and Knowledge* (New York: National Association of Social Workers, 1966), pp. 164–178.

afflicted) as directly, but they too felt that they had little autonomy or independence of action.

In obtaining departmental acceptance and support of the Midway Project, the researchers had indicated that interest was focused on work group organization and testing the effects of organizational change at that level only. However, it became clear that the management control of supervisors was so tight that if it were left unchecked, the measurement of client outcomes, for example, might reflect chiefly the uniformities attained by the top district office staff rather than reflecting possible differences in the outcomes of different forms of work group organization.

Departmental approval of the following modification of top-level management supervision in the Midway office was obtained. One assistant district office supervisor position was designated as having a supervisory function—that is, the incumbent had the authority and responsibility for initiating case reviews in all ten work groups and for reversing decisions of supervisors when necessary. The incumbent of the second assistant district office supervisor position was available to provide advice and assistance to any of the ten supervisors upon their request. The third assistant district office supervisor position was designated as an administrative assistant to the district office supervisor.

The reorganization of the top district office staff was an ad hoc effort to protect the integrity of the field experiment and no formal evaluation of this device was attempted. Although the top management of the district office continued to intervene in the case supervision process, this reorganization did have the effect of loosening the central control of the district office superstructure on the work groups and allowed for fuller manifestation of the effects of the different forms of work group organization.

The authorized relaxation of administrative-supervisory control in the Midway office may also have contributed to the dissatisfaction of the state review group with the level of conformance in the Midway office with regulations concerning eligibility and amount of assistance payments. However, the unfavorable view that the state review staff took of the administration of financial assistance in the Midway office was based on comparisons with audits made in other offices sometime before the Midway visit. The accelerated decline in morale, increasing hostility toward the department, rapidly mounting turnover, and the consequent increase in the difficulty of training staff and checking output—all of which were endemic throughout the department—were probably more important than changes brought about only within the Midway office.

With all the research staff's efforts to prevent contamination and dilution and to maintain the experimental input at full force, it is believed, that on balance the observed differences between conventional work groups and experimental teams in the criteria that were selected to measure outcomes—and especially those relating to client change—are less than might have been obtained in a better controlled or less perturbed environment. If this is the case, then the differences obtained represent a conservative expression of the true differences in the effects of the experimental and conventional forms of work group operation.

RELATION OF STAFF ATTITUDES TO STAFF PERFORMANCE

The three-stage hypothesis—(1) that the team form of organization will result in an increase in staff morale, (2) that higher morale will result in an increased volume of staff activity and service, and (3) that this in turn will be reflected in superior client outcomes—represented an effort to design the research in a way that would not only provide experimental data on outcomes but would also give at least some general information on the dynamics through which input in a public assistance agency is processed to produce given outcomes.

Of clients receiving service for one year, those served by the experimental teams did significantly better than those served by conventional work groups, as hypothesized. This was true under both high- and low-caseload conditions. As hypothesized, clients of work groups having both the team form of organization and low caseloads did better than groups having only one or neither of these advantages. The experimental input—the team form of organization—was more effective than the factor of caseload reduction in producing superior outcomes with the sample cases, and at a much lower direct financial cost.

The hypotheses on morale and productivity were, however, not supported. Members of the experimental teams did not exhibit significantly higher morale, nor did they produce a significantly higher volume of work. The findings therefore left the researchers with positive and substantial payoff findings on client outcomes, but with no information as to what went on in the difficult-to-observe process of service delivery that produced the desired results.

The researchers thereupon proceeded to examine the assumptions connecting the three major hypotheses. The relevant assumption underlying the first two was, of course, that high morale in public assistance field staff members is positively associated with high performance. Data from the studies of staff morale (Chapter 3) and staff performance (Chapter 4) made possible an analysis of the relationship of those two variables.[8]

Data for the independent variable—staff morale—were obtained from the returns on the job attitude portion of the "Employment and Job Attitude Questionnaire" from the Midway field staff at Time 1 near the beginning of the experiment and at Time 2 near the end. Work measurement data for the four months following the administration of the Time 1 "Employment and Job Attitude Questionnaire" and the four months preceding the administration of the Time 2 questionnaire were used for the dependent staff variable. Work assignment factors and selected personal characteristics of individual staff members were analyzed as intervening variables.

Positive associations were found between work performance and only two of twelve dimensions of work satisfaction—staff attitudes regarding work associates and supervisory practices.[9] Selected personal characteristics of workers were, however, found to be more positively related to volume of work performed than were most dimensions of work satisfaction.

Staff members who reported the largest volume of work performance were young, unmarried, white, and with only brief

---

8. This section is based on Thomas Carlsen, "A Study of Correlates of High Performance of Public Assistance Workers." Unpublished Ph.D. dissertation, University of Chicago, 1970.

9. Ibid., pp. 83–94. The correlation with work associates was significant at the .05 level and with supervisory practices at the .10 level, and was not significant for staff attitudes regarding the following ten dimensions: work organization, work efficacy, administrative effectiveness, supervisory managerial practices, communication effectiveness, personal development, employee benefits, job satisfaction, organization identification, and client service adequacy.

work experience in the department. (Generalizations regarding ethnicity in relation to some of the other characteristics are limited by the small number of older white and younger black persons in the Midway field staff.) Being young, members of this group were comparatively more energetic and achievement oriented; being unmarried, they were more geographically mobile; and being male and white they were not subject to sexual or racial discrimination and hence were likely to have greater opportunities for desirable employment elsewhere. As a result they tended to stay in the agency a shorter period of time than other members of the organization.

The young unmarried white males with brief agency tenure represented one polar group in the Midway office field staff. Older married black women with considerable departmental tenure, low performance rates, and high job attitude scores represented the other polar group. Remaining staff members with some of the characteristics of each of the polar groups had median production and morale scores.[10]

Research findings in the organizational theory literature on the relationship of job attitudes and work performance do not fit together in a way that provides clear and satisfying generalizations. Brayfield and Crockett, in one of the first major reviews of the relevant literature, concluded that there was no substantial relationship between employee attitudes and their job performance.[11] Herzberg and his associates took a cautious but more positive position in their review of some of the same studies and some different ones. They found that while the positive correlations obtained in many of the studies were low, taken together the studies provide enough evidence "to justify attention to attitudes as a factor in improving workers' output," and this is, of course, what was done in the present research.[12]

Vroom, in a subsequent review of the literature, selected

10. Production data for other district offices are not available, but returns on the "Employment and Job Attitude Questionnaire" indicate that the generalizations regarding personal characteristics and job attitudes formulated here for the Midway staff are applicable to the field staff of other district offices.

11. A. H. Brayfield and W. H. Crockett, "Employee Attitudes and Employee Performance," *Psychological Bulletin,* Vol. 52, No. 5 (September 1955), pp. 396–424.

twenty studies that met certain methodological criteria.[13] The median correlation between measures of job satisfaction and performance (more than one measure of performance was used in some studies) was only +.14 for twenty-three correlations. However, twenty of the twenty-three correlations were positive—a result that would occur by chance only once in one hundred times. Vroom states that job satisfaction is closely affected by the rewards that people derive from their jobs and that levels of performance are closely affected by the basis for attaining rewards. He concludes that "individuals are satisfied with their jobs to the extent to which their jobs provide them with what they desire, and they perform effectively in them to the extent that effective performance leads to the attainment of what they desire." [14]

Porter and Lawler characterize Vroom's (and Brayfield and Crockett's) theoretical position as a "path-goal approach" that treats job satisfaction as primarily a dependent rather than an independent variable.[15] Their theoretical model of the relationship of performance and satisfaction, which includes seven other antecedent, intervening, and subsequent variables, provides a basis for further consideration of the Midway findings of low morale and high productivity for one group of staff members (young single white men with little agency experience) and higher morale and lower productivity for those with the opposite characteristics. For the first group, high performance and the effort involved were not followed by the kind of perceived rewards that they were seeking—namely, a feeling of accomplishment in helping people, self-actualization, and appropriate organizational recognition. They tended to perceive unsuccessful outcomes of their efforts as being due in large part to departmental attitudes and policies that were hostile toward

---

12. Frederick Herzberg, Bernard Mausner, and Barbara Snyderman, *The Motivation to Work* (2d ed.; New York: John Wiley & Sons, 1959), p. 103.

13. V. H. Vroom, *Work and Motivation* (New York: John Wiley & Sons, 1964).

14. Ibid., p. 264.

15. Lyman W. Porter and Edward E. Lawler, III, *Managerial Attitudes and Performance* (Homewood, Ill.: Richard D. Irwin, 1968).

clients, and these perceptions led to negative attitudes toward the agency and early resignations.[16]

Although many of the second group of employees—the older married black women with considerable seniority in the agency—undoubtedly also valued self-actualization, personal development, and the service ideal, they apparently came to place greater emphasis on job security, status, promotion, and pay than did the first group. For example, the department's desire for a large volume of interviews was well known, but this group correctly perceived that the probabilities were low that organizational rewards would be chiefly and accurately related to high performance. The top administration valued high interviewing activity, but it appeared to place greater value on "loyalty"—meaning conformance—and even low performance was likely to result in the kind of rewards expected by those employees, although not necessarily at the desired level. The resulting job satisfaction was high enough, in the absence of other and better job opportunities, to hold incumbents in their jobs.

In light of this analysis, the assumption connecting the first and second major hypotheses—namely, that high morale would be associated with high productivity—was not supported by observations of the Midway office experience. Even if the data had shown that the team form of organization would stimulate higher morale, the immediately preceding discussion indicates that this would not necessarily have resulted in increased staff activity. The following analysis indicates that an assumption connecting the second and third major hypotheses—namely, that increased staff activity would be positively related to client outcomes—is likewise not supported by the data.

RELATION OF STAFF PERFORMANCE TO CLIENT OUTCOMES

The relationship between staff performance and field staff attitudes could be determined quite precisely because both of the

16. E. E. Smith, "The Effects of Clear and Unclear Role Expectations on Group Productivity and Defensiveness," *Journal of Abnormal and Social Psychology,* Vol. 55, No. 2 (September 1957), pp. 213–217.

variables involved are characteristics of the same study subject—namely, members of the field staff. However, analysis of the relationship between staff performance and client outcome is complicated by the fact that two different kinds of study subjects are involved, staff and clients. The high staff turnover endemic to the operation of public assistance agencies meant that most sample cases were served by more than one worker during the year. Moreover, in the instance of the experimental team, cases were assigned only to supervisors and service to the great majority of cases was provided concurrently by more than one member of the team. Reliance must therefore be placed on work group data for analyzing the relationship between services provided and client change scores. On the basis of the work group data presented in Chapters 3 and 4, it is now clear that the relevant assumption connecting the second and third major hypotheses—that volume of activity would be positively correlated with change scores—was not supported. One inference that can be drawn from this is that although the experimental team form of work group organization does not result in a greater volume of activity, it does tend to produce a distinctively effective distribution of available services.

To test this inference, the mean numbers of service units provided to sample cases served by the different types of work groups are shown in Table 31 by the class intervals, ranging from —1 to —7 through +5 and over into which their global change scores fell. The curves described by the data are U or J shaped (that is, there are lower mean numbers of service units for cases with scores of 0 through 4 than for cases with extreme scores) for the combined experimental cases and for three of the four subgroupings of experimental cases (family and individual cases in Plan A and family cases in Plan B). In contrast, the comparable data for neither the combined conventional cases nor any of the four subgroupings of conventional cases fall into that type of distribution.

The intent of the classification plan as developed for the experimental teams was to give priority in providing services to families and individuals exhibiting the kinds of needs and problems with which the supervisor decided his team could best deal.

While the approach of providing "intensive service to the hard core case" was rejected, we were also determined to avoid a mere "creaming" approach, which can mean withholding preventive and protective services. The classification plan and training process were devised to encourage team supervisors to

Table 31

Mean Number of Service Units Provided to Sample Cases, by Type of Work Group and Case[a]

	Change Score			
Type of Work Group and Case	−1 to −7	0 to +1	+2 to +4	+5 and over[b]
All cases	4.2	3.9	4.5	5.0
Combined conventional work groups	3.5	3.8	5.4	4.3
Combined experimental teams	4.8	3.9	3.8	5.5
Plan A				
Conventional work groups				
Total cases	2.6	2.9	2.8	2.8
Family cases	2.3	2.4	2.9	—
Individual cases	3.1	4.1	2.7	2.8
Experimental teams				
Total cases	2.9	2.5	2.3	3.2
Family cases	2.0	1.4	2.1	2.5
Individual cases	4.8	4.1	2.7	3.7
Plan B				
Conventional work groups				
Total cases	5.2	4.9	7.1	5.4
Family cases	4.2	4.0	5.5	3.7
Individual cases	5.6	5.5	9.0	5.9
Experimental teams				
Total cases	6.9	5.2	5.4	6.2
Family cases[c]	6.8	3.0	3.8	8.1
Individual cases	6.9	7.6	7.2	5.1

[a] The numbers of each type of case are given in Table 25.

[b] The highest positive score achieved was +10.

[c] F=3.27, 3 d.f., 3b, p<.05.

be responsive to the needs of clients found to be in threatening or emergency situations while at the same time focusing available resources on the most responsive families and individuals. Implementation of this two-pronged approach appears to be quite clearly reflected in the bimodal distribution of service units provided by experimental teams along the axis of the mean change scores for their clients. The fairly large concentrations of services on cases served by experimental teams that showed negative change reflects both the large number of emergency and other threatening situations to which the Midway population was subject and the more responsive efforts of the team to at least moderate the rate of regression in the families and individuals involved.

For cases with global change scores above +1, the association of the number of service units provided and the global change scores achieved is positive for combined experimental team cases and negative for combined conventional work group cases. These data support the explanation that the superior outcomes of sample cases served by experimental teams result from the fact that the services provided by the experimental teams were more effectively distributed among the cases for which they were responsible.

This explanation is given some confirmation by a one-way analysis of variance within the mean number of service units provided to cases grouped by their change scores. Of the fifteen such distributions presented in Table 31, eight are for the basic types of work group cases. (The remaining seven distributions are for "combined" or "total" data derived from the distributions for the eight basic types of work group cases.) The only significant variance among means is for family cases served by experimental teams in Plan B, but the variance among means for individual cases served by experimental teams in Plan A borders on the significant. Reference to Table 26 (page 136) shows that it was the same two basic types of cases and the only basic types for which significantly superior outcomes—as measured by global change scores—were demonstrated. The variance for none of the four conventional types comes close to being significant.

Although this evidence is both limited and indirect, it suggests that the experimental teams made planful and—as it turned out—more effective use of their manpower resources than did the conventional work groups. The team supervisors were in a position to make decisions for every case as to what was to be attempted and how much work was to be done by whom and in what order. Direct observations indicated that this is what was done and that the case-classification plans were used by the team supervisors as guides to planning and carrying out treatment.

No claim is made concerning the completeness, precision, or certainty of knowledge gained concerning what went on in the service delivery system to produce the outcomes observed. It seems clear that the intervening variables of morale and volume of work were not determinative. It also seems plausible that the opportunity for and the exercise of flexible and rational control of staff resources by team supervisors represented an important contribution to the superior outcomes achieved by the experimental teams.

The Midway Project findings, like those of any field experiment, relate to a given experiment at a specific time. To check the reliability of laboratory experiments through replication is standard procedure. Whether all or part of the Midway experiment should be repeated is of course a matter of research strategy and opportunity. The following observations are offered on the assumption that the Midway findings are based on the most reliable and valid observations available on the phenomena to which they are addressed.

THE SOCIAL WORK SUPERVISORY MODEL

The development of bureaucracies performing functions now perceived as social welfare preceded the development of social work as a profession in this country at the turn of the twentieth century. An important aspect of the struggle of the early social welfare reformers was reform of the poorhouses, workhouses, prisons, mental hospitals, and other bureaucracies whose operations were seen to be harmful to the people with whom they were in contact. Social work developed as a bureaucratized profession, but only after organizations such as community service societies and family and children's welfare agencies had appeared whose goals were congruent with those of the profession-to-be. The movement for the establishment of social work education was sparked and energized by social agency resources. Conversely, employment in the same agencies represented the labor market for early graduates of the new schools of social work. The faculties of the new graduate schools were drawn in large part from the supervisory and executive staff of the social agencies that had stimulated and supported the development of the schools. The master-apprentice form of supervision and training was carried over into the schools as "supervisory fieldwork" and became an integral and important part of social work education.

Through a kind of continuing and reflexive action, the tutorial or coaching relationship that characterized the interaction between the field supervisor and social work student was carried back into practice in the form of a social work supervisory model in which the supervisor had the dual functions of (1) teacher responsible for the professional development of his supervisees and (2) administrative control officer, responsible for protecting the organization and its clients by monitoring the performance of supervisees and so obtaining conformance to agency policies and standards.

During the Great Depression of the 1930s, the social work profession claimed as its responsibility the administration of financial assistance to the unemployed. This claim was recognized sufficiently to permit the profession to impose the social work supervisory model on the work group organization of state emergency relief and public assistance agencies, along with such other impediments as the means test for the determination of eligibility and the budgetary deficit method of determining the amount of assistance grants.

The social work supervisory model as developed and used in highly professionalized social work agencies—that is, agencies where policy is subject and amenable to the values of the social work profession and where social workers are in a position to define program and provide services—has been reasonably viable and functional, especially when it has been updated and modified. The improvement of the traditional social work supervisory model includes recognition of the conflict involved in the dual role of the supervisor, more specific and appropriate provision for the early granting of professional autonomy, establishment of the distinction between supervision and consultation, and the provision of consultation to all staff who desire to use it.

The state public assistance agencies in this country have, however, never been highly professionalized, and the ill-fitting social work supervisory model has been subject to increasing distortion. Some of the specific aspects of the distortion of this model subsequent to its uncritical and unfortunate adoption by the public assistance establishment were specified earlier in the researchers' criticism of the conventional way of utilizing public assistance staff.[17]

In the conventional public assistance work group the responsibilities of the supervisor and the worker are differentiated chiefly on a hierarchical basis around the central function of the organization—that is, the provision of financial assistance. Verbal recognition continues to be given to the responsibility of supervisors for the "professional" development of their supervisees, regardless of whcther the workers have the prerequisite educational background, and many conscientious supervisors make some effort to oblige.

In practice, however, especially in urban and other high-pressure public assistance offices, the staff development functions of the supervisor tend to be honored more in the breach than in the observance. Among the reasons for this failure are the inability of some supervisors to carry out this function because of the press of administrative work; their lack of knowledge, skills, or personal aptitude; or other incapacities for staff development. A specialized in-service training and staff development program represents one kind of response by public assistance agencies to the need to supplement and strengthen supervisors' contributions in this area.

The literature on training, like that on recruitment and utiliza-

---

17. *See* Chapter 1, pp. 3–4. *See also* Peter M. Blau and W. Richard Scott, *Formal Organizations: A Comparative Approach* (San Francisco: Chandler Publishing Co., 1962).

tion of personnel for public assistance programs, has tended to assume the continuance of the conventional professional supervisory model. Focus has been on programs for raising the skills of workers without professional education to the point at which their performance, as observed and judged by supervisory and related personnel, would appear to be as similar as possible to that of professionally qualified social workers.[18] For example, Meyer has attempted to differentiate the structure, content, and method of in-service training for public welfare workers from those of the professional education of social workers, keeping in view a commitment to the best possible treatment of public welfare clients. Even this most valiant effort foundered because she felt constrained to accept the conventional professional supervisory model of the public welfare bureaucracy for differentiating the roles of supervisors and workers.[19]

Even before the passage of the Social Security Act in 1935, the shortage of public assistance staff with the educational requirements for full professional social work status meant that the traditional professional social work supervisory model was never a real possibility for this field. The effort to force a fit by instituting in-service training programs has fostered an unsuccessful pseudoprofessional model. Few public assistance agencies have proved themselves equal to the task of developing viable income maintenance and service programs, to say nothing of preempting a function of institutions of higher learning by substituting prolonged in-service training programs for professional education. Their training efforts are being curtailed, not necessarily because of the belated recognition that they were ill conceived, but rather because it is increasingly evident that they are not effective. The continuing high rate of staff turnover in beginning positions in public assistance agencies, along with constriction in funds, has made abundantly clear the wastefulness of costly in-service training programs for large numbers of short-term employees.

---

18. *See,* for example Virginia Tannar, *Selected Social Work Concepts for Public Welfare Workers* (Washington, D.C.: U.S. Department of Health, Education & Welfare, 1965).

19. Carol H. Meyer, *Staff Development in Public Welfare Agencies* (New York: Columbia University Press, 1966).

FUTURE WORK GROUP ORGANIZATION

The Midway experiment did not demonstrate that the team form of organization reduced staff turnover, but that it was more effective with respect to client change than the conventional form of work group organization under conditions of high turnover.

Not all staff turnover is necessarily dysfunctional for organizations or for the careers of the individuals immediately involved. Short-term employment of low-paid staff members performing work requiring little training or experience can be part of rational employment practices if it is planned to meet the needs of employees as well as employers. Some recent college graduates and other young people have found one or two years of employment in a public assistance agency to be a useful form of career-testing. Too often, however, the experience has been negative because the demands of the job were too high initially and the prospective rewards too low. The flexible and progressive use of task assignments in the experimental team form of organization would make possible less trying methods of inducting inexperienced workers and better accommodation to the needs of public assistance agencies.

Since the inception of the Midway Project, the differential use of public assistance personnel has been the subject of much discussion, some research, and little, if any, reported experimentation. During the 1960s a considerable amount of research was conducted on the utilization of manpower in the fields of health, mental health, and education, as well as in social welfare settings.[20] Widespread agreement was reached that professional staff alone could not meet the need for increased services in these fields and that increased use would have to be made of paraprofessional workers. Indeed in some quarters advocacy of the paraprofessional or "new careerist" reached crusade proportions. Yet in spite of a flurry of literature on the paraprofessional in the

---

20. A review of the literature on the utilization of social welfare personnel in general appears in Robert L. Barker and Thomas L. Briggs, "Trends in the Utilization of Social Work Personnel: An Evaluative Research of the Literature," Report No. 2 (New York: National Association of Social Workers, June 1966). (Mimeographed.)

late 1960s and continuing analysis of the role of the professional social worker, little research has appeared that is directed to the ways in which the varying contributions of professional and paraprofessional staff are presently interrelated and might be improved. With the rather abrupt tightening of the social welfare labor market in the late 1960s, the interrelationship of the various levels of manpower may come to be of greater interest to those involved in the employment of paraprofessionals as well as of professional social workers.

The abatement of bureaucratic and professional anxiety in the late 1960s concerning manpower shortages in social welfare occurred not because of any unexpected increase in the supply of qualified social workers or any diminution in the need for welfare services as perceived by professionals and other informed persons, but rather because of developing financial stringencies in governmental and other funds allocated for social services. In the early 1960s governmental sources estimated that the shortage of social workers with master's degrees would by 1970 be in the order of 100,000.[21] The gross discrepancy between this estimate of need and the true demand in 1970 was visible even before the end of the decade.[22]

Nationwide surveys of social welfare employment in the United States were completed for 1950 and 1960 but, unfortunately, not for 1970, so that country-wide data on the level of employment and the state of the labor market in this field are not available for recent years. A major development in the manpower picture during the 1960s was a spurt in the development of undergraduate social welfare curricula. This was followed by high unemployment of professional social workers starting in the late 1960s. Although national data continue to be unavailable, it seems likely that the demand for more highly qualified social workers will continue to be greater than for other social welfare personnel and that the extent of this unmet demand will vary positively with the educational requirements for unfilled positions.

---

21. Alvin L. Schorr, "Need for Trained Social Work Staff: A Ten-Year Goal," *Social Security Bulletin,* Vol. 24, No. 8 (August, 1961), pp. 11–13.

22. Sydney Zimbalist and Claire M. Anderson, *Social Welfare Manpower* (Chicago: Welfare Council of Metropolitan Chicago, 1968), p. 19.

Regardless of the vagaries of politics and the rather poorly organized social work labor market, the economic necessity of improving the differential utilization of personnel in the social welfare field as a whole is likely to persist. Experimentation on differential use of social welfare personnel may well go in the direction of testing a variety of team and other models of work group organization in a wide range of social welfare settings. This and other research can be more effectively planned, conducted, and utilized when better information becomes available on the total social welfare manpower system. The achievement of an adequate information system—that is, one providing comprehensive current data on manpower and other factors in the social welfare system—is required for effective manpower planning in social welfare.

A major change in the public assistance picture, which seems likely to have a longer-run impact on staff utilization than shifts in the labor market, is the separation of financial services from other welfare services. The implementation of policy promulgated by the Department of Health, Education, and Welfare may be expedited by legislative enactment of proposals for increasing the involvement of the federal government in the financing and administration of a family assistance program. The separation of financial assistance from welfare service functions of public assistance programs will reveal the sorry state of the welfare service component in most states and localities and the need for their development.

The fact that the experimental teams were shown to be superior in effecting better client outcomes and the conventional work groups were superior in adhering to agency regulations concerning eligibility for providing financial assistance suggests that these differences in outcomes may be exploited in efforts to achieve various specified goals. It seems likely that the difficulties experienced by the Midway field staff in providing welfare services would have been greatly reduced and the superiority of the experimental teams in performing this function would have been even more evident if financial services had been provided by another staff. However, this belief and that concerning the feasibility of using teams under conditions of low as well as high staff turnover have not yet been demonstrated in the public assistance setting and both remain to be tested.

BIBLIOGRAPHY

Anderson, Claire M. "Work Group Communication Among Welfare Workers." Unpublished Ph.D. dissertation, University of Chicago School of Social Service Administration, 1966.

———, Schwartz, Edward E., and Vishwanathan, Narayan. "Approaches to the Analysis of Social Service Systems." *PPBS and Social Welfare.* Chicago: University of Chicago School of Social Service Administration, 1970.

Anderson, Odin, and Feldman, Jacob J. *Family Medical Costs and Voluntary Health Insurance: A Nationwide Survey.* New York: McGraw-Hill Book Co., 1956.

The Area Development Project, Monographs I, II, and III. Vancouver, B.C.: United Community Services of the Greater Vancouver Area, 1968–69.

Baehr, Melany E., and Renck, Richard. "The Definition and Measurement of Employee Morale," *Administrative Science Quarterly,* Vol. 3, No. 2 (September 1958), pp. 157–184.

Barker, Robert L., and Briggs, Thomas L. "Trends in the Utilization of Social Work Personnel: An Evaluative Research of the Literature." Research Report No. 2. New York: National Association of Social Workers, June 1966. (Mimeographed.)

Behling, John H. "An Experimental Study to Measure the Effectiveness of Casework Services." Unpublished Ph.D. dissertation, Ohio University, 1961.

Blau, Peter M., and Scott, W. Richard. *Formal Organizations: A Comparative Approach.* San Francisco: Chandler Publishing Co., 1962.

Blenkner, Margaret, et al. *Serving the Aging: An Experiment in Social Work and Public Health Nursing.* New York: Community Service Society, 1964.

Brayfield, A. H., and Crockett, W. H. "Employee Attitudes and Employee Performance." *Psychological Bulletin,* Vol. 52, No. 5 (September 1955), pp. 396–424.

Burgess, M. Elaine, and Price, Daniel O. *An American Dependency Challenge.* Chicago: American Public Welfare Association, 1963.

Carlsen, Thomas. "A Study of Correlates of High Performance of Public Assistance Workers." Unpublished Ph.D. dissertation, University of Chicago School of Social Service Administration, 1970.

Chaskel, Ruth. "Public Social Policy and Casework Services in Public Welfare," *Social Work,* Vol. 4, No. 3 (July 1959), pp. 27–34.

Cohen, Wilbur J., and Bernard, Sydney E. *The Prevention and Reduction of Dependency.* Ann Arbor, Mich.: Washtenaw County Department of Social Welfare, 1961.

"Facts, Fallacies and Future: A Study of the Aid to Dependent Children Program of Cook County, Illinois." New York: Greenleigh Associates, 1960. (Mimeographed.)

Geismar, Ludwig. *Patterns of Change in Problem Families.* St. Paul, Minn.: Family-Centered Project, 1959.

———. "The Rutgers Family Life Improvement Project and Other Outcome Studies." Unpublished paper presented at the National Conference on Social Welfare, Chicago, Ill., May 1970.

———, and Ayres, Beverly. *Measuring Family Functioning.* St. Paul, Minn.: Family-Centered Project, 1960.

———, and Krisberg, Jane. *The Forgotten Neighborhood: Site of an Early Skirmish in the War on Poverty.* Metuchen, N.J.: Scarecrow Press, 1967.

Glasser, Melvin A. "Extension of Public Welfare Medical Care: Issues of Social Policy," *Social Work,* Vol. 10, No. 4 (October 1965), pp. 3–9.

Gripton, James M. "A Study of the Relationship of Job Attitudes and Work Organization of Public Assistance Workers." Unpublished Ph.D. dissertation, University of Toronto, 1967.

Heiland, Robert E., and Wallace, J. Richardson. *Work Sampling.* New York: McGraw-Hill Book Co., 1957.

Hellenbrand, Shirley C. "Client Value Orientations: Implications for Diagnosis and Treatment," *Social Casework,* Vol. 42, No. 4 (April 1961), pp. 163–169.

Herzberg, Frederick, Mausner, Bernard, and Snyderman, Barbara Bloch. *Job Attitudes: Review of Research and Opinion.* Pittsburgh: Psychological Service of Pittsburgh, 1957.

———. *The Motivation to Work.* 2d ed.; New York: John Wiley & Sons, 1964.

Herzog, Elizabeth. *Some Guide Lines to Evaluative Research.* Washington, D.C.: U.S. Department of Health, Education & Welfare, 1951.

Hetzler, Stanley A. "A Scale for Measuring Case Severity and Case Movement in Public Assistance," *Social Casework,* Vol. 44, No. 5 (May 1963), pp. 445–451.

Heyman, Margaret. "A Study of Effective Use of Social Workers in a Hospital: Selected Findings and Conclusions," *Social Service Review,* Vol. 35, No. 4 (December 1961), pp. 414–429.

Hollingshead, August B., and Redlich, Frederick C. *Social Class and Mental Illness: A Community Study.* New York: John Wiley & Sons, 1958.

Hudson, Walter H. "The Unit Clerk System." Chicago: Cook County Department of Public Aid, 1966. (Mimeographed.)

Hull, R. L., and Kolsted, Arthur. "Morale on the Job," in Goodwin Watson, ed., *Civilian Morale.* Boston: Houghton Mifflin, 1942.

Hunt, Joseph McVicker, and Kogan, Leonard S. *Measuring Results in Social Casework.* New York: Family Service Association of America, 1950.

Kahn, J. P., MD. "Attitudes Toward Recipients of Public Assistance," *Social Casework,* Vol. 36, No. 8 (October 1955), pp. 359–364.

Kermish, Irving, and Kuslin, Frank. "Why High Turnover? Staff Losses in a County Welfare Department," *Public Welfare,* Vol. 27, No. 2 (April 1969), pp. 134–140.

Kilpatrick, Dee. "Health-Related Services to Low-Income Pregnant Clients: A Study of Health Attitudes and Service Delivery in Public Welfare. Unpublished Ph.D. dissertation, University of Chicago School of Social Service Administration, August 1969.

Kuhl, P. H. *The Family Center Project and Action Research on Socially Deprived Families.* Copenhagen, Denmark: Danish National Institute of Social Research, 1969.

Lundberg, George. *Social Research.* New York: Longman's Green & Co., 1946.

Macdonald, Mary E. "Compatibility of Theory and Method: An Analysis of Six Studies," in Ann W. Shyne, ed., *Use of Judgments as Data in Social Work Research.* New York: National Association of Social Workers, 1959.

Marin, Rosa C. "A Comprehensive Program for Multi-Problem Families," *Report on a Four-Year Controlled Experiment.* Rio Piedras, Puerto Rico: Institute of Caribbean Studies, University of Puerto Rico, 1969.

May, Edgar. *Our Costly Dilemma.* Buffalo: *Buffalo Evening News,* 1960.

———. "Social Work Research: A Perspective," in Norman Polansky, ed., *Social Work Research.* Chicago: University of Chicago Press, 1960.

McCabe, A. R. *The Pursuit of Promise: A Study of the Intellectually Superior Child in a Socially Deprived Area.* New York: Community Service Society, 1967.

McClusky, H. Y. C., and Strayer, Floyd J. "Reactions of Teachers to the Teaching Situation: A Study of Job Satisfaction," *School Review,* Vol. 48, No. 7 (October 1940), pp. 612–623.

McLeod, Donna, and Hylton, Lydia F. *An Evaluation of a Method for Administering In-Service Training in Aid to Dependent Children.* Ann Arbor: University of Michigan School of Social Work, 1958.

Meyer, Carol H. *Staff Development in Public Welfare Agencies.* New York: Columbia University Press, 1966.

Meyer, Henry J., Borgatta, Edgar F., and Jones, Wyatt C. *Girls at Vocational High.* New York: Russell Sage Foundation, 1965.

Moore, David G., and Renck, Richard. "The Professional Employee in Industry," *Journal of Business,* Vol. 38, No. 1 (January 1965), pp. 58–66.

Muller, Charlotte. "Income and the Receipt of Medical Care," *American Journal of Public Health,* Vol. 40, No. 4 (April 1965), pp. 510–521.

New Careers Newsletter. New York: New York University, New Careers Development Center.

New York City Department of Social Service Collaborative Demonstration Project. New York: Community Service Society of New York, in preparation.

Perlman, Helen Harris. *Casework: A Problem-Solving Process.* Chicago: University of Chicago Press, 1957.

Porter, Lyman W., and Lawler, Edward E., III. *Managerial Attitudes and Performance.* Homewood, Ill.: Richard D. Irwin, 1968.

The Red Door: A Report on Neighborhood Services. Vancouver, B.C.: United Community Services of the Greater Vancouver Area, 1968–69.

Reid, William J., and Shyne, Ann W. *Brief and Extended Casework.* New York: Columbia University Press, 1969.

Rettig, Salomon, and Pasamanick, Benjamin. "Status, Work Satisfaction, and Variables of Work Satisfaction of Psychiatric Social Workers," *Mental Hygiene,* Vol. 44, No. 1 (January 1960), pp. 48–54.

Richan, Willard C. "A Theoretical Scheme for Determining Roles of Professional and Nonprofessional Personnel," *Social Work,* Vol. 6, No. 4 (October 1961), pp. 22–28.

Ripple, Lilian. *Motivation, Capacity and Opportunity: Studies in Casework Theory and Practice.* Chicago: University of Chicago School of Social Service Administration, 1964.

———. "Plans for Obtaining Judgment Data," in Ann W. Shyne, ed., *Use of Judgments as Data in Social Work Research.* New York: National Association of Social Workers, 1959.

Rosten, Leo. *Captain Newman, M.D.* New York: Harper & Row, 1962.

Sample, William C. "A Study of Client Change in Public Welfare." Unpublished doctoral dissertation, University of Chicago School of Social Service Administration, 1968.

Schwartz, Edward E. "Adoption and Foster Home Costs," *Cost Analysis in Child Welfare Services.* Washington, D.C.: U.S. Government Printing Office, 1958.

———. *Cost Analysis and Performance Budgeting in Child Welfare and Public Assistance, State of Maine.* New York: Laurin Hyde & Associates, 1962.

———. "Strategies for Research in Public Welfare Administration: The Field Experiment," *Trends in Social Work Practice and Knowledge.* New York: National Association of Social Workers, 1966.

———, and Sample, William C. "First Findings from Midway," *Social Service Review,* Vol. 41, No. 2 (June 1967), pp. 113–151.

Schorr, Alvin L. "Need for Trained Social Work Staff: A Ten-Year Goal," *Social Security Bulletin,* Vol. 24, No. 8 (August 1961), pp. 11–13.

Shyne, Ann W. "Evaluation of Results in Social Work," *Social Work,* Vol. 8, No. 4 (October 1963), pp. 26–33.

———, and Kogan, Leonard S. "A Study of the Components of Movement," *Social Casework,* Vol. 39, No. 6 (June 1958), pp. 333-342.

Siegal, Sidney. *Non-Parametric Statistics for the Behavioral Sciences.* New York: McGraw-Hill Book Co., 1956.

Simon, Herbert A., Divine, W. R., Cooper, E. M., and Chernin, Milton. *Determining Workloads for Professional Staff in a Public Welfare Agency.* Berkeley: University of California, Bureau of Public Administration, 1941.

Smith, E. E. "The Effects of Clear and Unclear Role Expectations on Group Productivity and Defensiveness," *Journal of Abnormal and Social Psychology,* Vol. 55, No. 2 (September 1957), pp. 213–217.

Spergel, Irving, and Mundy, Richard. "Social Facts About Woodlawn." Chicago: University of Chicago School of Social Service Administration, 1961. (Mimeographed.)

"Staff Organization in Public Welfare and Client Change: A Reanalysis of the Midway Data," *School of Social Service Administration Newsletter,* Vol. 14, No. 2 (April 1967), pp. 26–27.

"A Study of Marin County, California: Building Services into a Public Assistance Program Can Pay Off." Sacramento: California State Department of Social Welfare, undated.

Tannar, Virginia. *Selected Social Work Concepts for Public Welfare Workers.* Washington, D.C.: U.S. Department of Health, Education & Welfare, 1965.

Thomas, Edwin J., and McLeod, Donna L. *In-Service Training and Reduced Workloads: Experiments in a State Department of Welfare.* New York: Russell Sage Foundation, 1960.

Tollen, William B. *Study of Staff Losses in Child Welfare and Family Service Agencies.* Washington, D.C.: U.S. Government Printing Office, 1960.

Tyler, Ralph W. "Future Prospects of the Behavioral Sciences," in Ozzie G. Simmons, ed., *The Behavioral Sciences: Problems and Prospects.* Boulder, Colo.: Institute of Behavioral Science, 1964.

U.S. Department of Labor, Bureau of Labor Statistics. *Salaries and Working Conditions of Social Welfare Manpower 1960.* New York: National Social Welfare Assembly, 1961.

Uno, Hirobumi. "Work Patterns of Work Groups in the Administration of Public Assistance." Unpublished Ph.D. dissertation, University of Chicago School of Social Service Administration, 1966.

Vroom, V. H. *Work and Motivation.* New York: John Wiley & Sons, 1964.

Walker, Nigel. *Morale in the Civil Service: A Study of the Desk Worker.* Edinburgh, Scotland: Edinburgh University Press, 1961.

Weinberger, Paul E. "Job Satisfaction and Staff Retention in Social Work." *NASW News,* Vol. 15, No. 2 (March 1970), pp. 10, 23–24.

Wiltse, Kermit T. "Social Casework Services in the Aid to Dependent Children Program," *Social Service Review,* Vol. 28, No. 2 (June 1954), pp. 173–185.

Wolfbein, Seymour. "Technicians and the Utilization of Professional Manpower," *Proceedings of a Conference on the Utilization of Scientific and Professional Manpower.* New York: Columbia University Press, 1954.

Zimbalist, Sidney, and Anderson, Claire M. *Social Welfare Manpower.* Chicago: Welfare Council of Metropolitan Chicago, 1968.

3M—PD—5/72